GATES TO BUDDHIST PRACTICE

Gates to Buddhist Practice

Essential Teachings of a Tibetan Master

REVISED EDITION

Chagdud Tulku

PADMA PUBLISHING

2001

Published by
Padma Publishing
P.O. Box 279
Junction City, CA 96048-0279

© Padma Publishing 1993
© Revised Edition 2001

Reprinted 2006, 2012

Printed in the United States of America

Library of Congress Cataloging-in-Publication Data

Chagdud Tulku
Gates to Buddhist practice: essential teachings
of a Tibetan master / Chagdud Tulku.—
Rev. ed.
p. cm.
Includes index.

ISBN-13: 978-1-881847-14-4

1. Religious life—Buddhism. 2. Buddhism

BQ5395.C43 2001

294.3'449—dc21   00-52404

Contents

Editors' Preface

GATES TO BUDDHIST PRACTICE, the first volume of The Living Dharma Series: Oral Teachings of Chagdud Tulku, presents traditional Tibetan Buddhist wisdom to Western readers in His Eminence Chagdud Tulku Rinpoche's uniquely accessible style, interweaving stories from his native Tibet with a step-by-step exploration of the foundation and essence of Vajrayana Buddhism.

Son of Dawa Drolma, one of Tibet's most renowned female lamas, Chagdud Rinpoche received extensive training from many great lamas and belongs to the last generation of teachers to have inherited the vast wealth of Tibetan Buddhist teachings and methods before the Chinese Communist consolidation of power in Tibet. In 1959, he was forced into exile and, during the two decades that followed, served the Tibetan community in India and Nepal as lama and physician. He also aided in refugee resettlement, as well as the artistic development of new monasteries.

Abbot of Chagdud Gonpa in Tibet—a centuries-old monastery and one of the few to survive the Chinese Communist invasion—Rinpoche came to the United States in 1979. In 1983 he established Chagdud Gonpa Foundation, which has centers throughout the United States, South America, and Europe. Rinpoche now lives at Khadro Ling, in Três Coroas, Brazil, Chagdud

Gonpa's main center in South America. His wisdom and compassion, which derive from a treasury of human experience, scholarly training, and profound meditative insight, permeate his presentation of the Buddhadharma—a presentation that, rich with metaphor, transcends cultural and religious barriers, and spirals through the extensive body of Buddhist teachings to their very heart.

Since Rinpoche came to the West, thousands of spiritual practitioners have gained insight into mind's nature through his instruction on the Vajrayana. A master of the most profound teachings of the Buddhist path, the Great Perfection (Dzogchen), he is committed to making the full range of Vajrayana methods available to Western students. His teachings, imbued with the Great Perfection perspective and transmitted with warmth and humor, reveal to those who are receptive a glimpse of their intrinsic awareness.

Most of Rinpoche's public talks have been tape-recorded. The Living Dharma Series consists of edited transcripts of those teachings. In *Gates to Buddhist Practice,* Rinpoche speaks of why we suffer and how we can eliminate the causes of suffering to create ultimate freedom for ourselves and others. He presents a multitude of methods for working with the mind in daily life; for reducing anger, attachment, ignorance, jealousy, and pride; for practicing effortful and effortless meditation; and for developing wisdom and compassion. Readers will find spiritual truths that are relevant to and of immediate benefit in their daily lives, truths that when applied with sincerity will produce unequivocal changes in their own minds and in their interactions with others. The book also contains an introduction to the Vajrayana, the "lightning path," which can be pursued with a qualified teacher.

The teachings presented here serve as an introduction to Chagdud Rinpoche's presentation of the Buddhadharma. Individual chapters are self-contained, yet the book proceeds through a progression of ideas, themes, and practices. The depth of these teachings will become increasingly apparent upon repeated readings, but more so through the application of the principles taught. *Gates to Buddhist Practice* is a book not only about the philosophy of the Buddhist religion, but also about Buddhist practice, the methods taught by the Buddha Shakyamuni 2,500 years ago that have produced profound transformation in the minds of those who have diligently applied them.

May this book be the cause of liberation for all who read it, and may all find freedom from the cycles of suffering and awaken to their mind's true nature.

Editors' Preface to
the Revised Edition

SINCE ITS PUBLICATION in 1993, *Gates to Buddhist Practice* has illuminated themes in Buddhist thought for new and experienced practitioners alike, and has provided instruction to people of all spiritual backgrounds.

Until his passing in 2002, His Eminence Chagdud Tulku Rinpoche continued to teach in North and South America, and met with thousands of sincere, enthusiastic, and sometimes skeptical students. The questions inspired by these teachings form the basis of the material added to this revised edition. Rinpoche provides insight into formal meditation practice as well as the integration of spiritual methods into daily life. Thus new readers will receive the benefit of other students' efforts to understand the teachings and clarify their practical concerns with an authentic lama.

In addition, the original index has been revised and a glossary compiled. Both will be helpful to new students and those familiar with the dharma, particularly those who intend to use this book as a reference or study guide.

Acknowledgments

IT IS BECAUSE of His Eminence Chagdud Tulku Rinpoche's tireless compassion, kindness, and commitment to the liberation of beings that these teachings have become available.

Great appreciation is due to the translators and interpreters of these teachings: Lama Chökyi Nyima (Richard Barron), who translated from the Tibetan, and Lama Tsering Everest, Lama Shenpen Drolma (Lisa Leghorn), and Chagdud Khadro (Jane Tromge), who interpreted Rinpoche's new and unique English for Western audiences.

Gratitude is extended to Lama Tsultrim Palmo (Mary Racine), Kimberley Snow, and Barry Spacks, who worked tirelessly as a team with Lama Shenpen to enable *Gates to Buddhist Practice* to emerge from the transcript pages, as well as to Gina Phelan, Anna Smith, and Linda Baer for their help in preparing this revised edition. Appreciation is due as well to all those who contributed invaluable help at various stages of the project.

PART I

*Discovering the Path
to Freedom*

1

Turning the Wheel

WHY DO WE NEED a spiritual path? We live in a busy age, our lives overflow with activities—some joyous, some painful, some satisfying, some not. Why take time to do spiritual practice?

A story is often told about a man from the northern region of Tibet who decided to go on a pilgrimage with his friends to the Potala Palace, the Dalai Lama's home in Lhasa, a very holy place. It was the trip of a lifetime.

In those days, there were no cars or vehicles of any kind in that region, and people journeyed on foot or by horse. It took a long time to get anywhere, and it was dangerous to go very far, as many thieves and robbers preyed on unsuspecting travelers. For these reasons, most people stayed in their home area all their lives. Most had never seen a house; they lived in black tents woven from yak hair.

When this particular group of pilgrims finally arrived in Lhasa, the man from the north was awed by the multi-storied Potala Palace with its many windows and the spectacular view of the town from within. He poked his head through a narrow slit window to get a better look, craning it left and right as he gazed at the sights below. When his friends called for him to leave, he jerked his head back, but couldn't get it out of the window. He became very nervous, pulling this way and that.

Finally he decided that he was really stuck. So he said to his friends, "Go home without me. Tell my family the bad news is that I died, but the good news is that I died in the Potala Palace. What better place to die?"

His friends were also very simpleminded, so without thinking much about it, they agreed and left. Some time later, the palace shrine keeper came along and asked, "Beggar, what are you doing here?"

"I'm dying," he answered.

"Why do you think you are dying?"

"Because my head is stuck."

"How did you get it in?"

"I put it in like this."

The shrine keeper replied, "So pull it out the same way!"

The man did as the shrine keeper suggested, and he was free.

Like this man, if we can see how we're caught, we can break free and help others to do the same. But first we need to understand how we got where we are.

Throughout life, though each of us seeks and sometimes finds happiness, it is always temporary; we cannot make it last. It's as if we keep shooting arrows, but at the wrong target. To find long-lasting happiness, we need to change our target: to focus on eradicating the suffering of ourselves and others, not only temporarily, but permanently.

The mind is the source of both our suffering and our happiness. It can be used positively to create benefit or negatively to create harm. Although every being's fundamental nature is beginningless, deathless purity—what we call buddha nature—we don't recognize it. Instead, we are controlled by the whims of ordinary mind, which leads us up and down, around and about, producing good and bad, pleasant and painful thoughts. Meanwhile, we plant a seed with every thought, word, and action. As surely as the seed of a poisonous plant bears poisonous fruit or a medicinal plant a cure, harmful actions produce suffering and beneficial actions, happiness.

Our actions become causes, and from causes naturally come results. Anything put into motion produces a corresponding motion. Throw a pebble into a pond and waves flow out in rings, strike the bank, and return. So it is when thoughts move: they flow out, then return. When the results of those thoughts come back, we feel like helpless victims: we're innocently leading our lives—why are all these things happening to us? The answer is that the rings are coming back to the center. This is karma.

Ordinary mind is vacillating and full of turbulence. Without any power to control it and its effects on body and speech, we're up, then down, then back and forth; we're riding a roller coaster of reality.

It is as though we start a wheel turning, give it another spin every time we react, and find ourselves caught in its perpetual motion. This ever-cycling experience of reality, in all of its variations, continues lifetime after lifetime. This is the endlessness of samsara, of cyclic existence. We don't understand that we're experiencing results that we ourselves have brought into being, and that our reactions ceaselessly produce more causes and more results.

Because we have created our own predicament, it's up to us to change it. Someone with matted, greasy hair looking in a mirror can't clean himself up by wiping the mirror. Someone with a bile disease will have a distorted sense of color and will see a white surface—whether a distant snow mountain or a piece of white cloth—as slightly yellow. The only way to correct that flawed vision is to cure the disease. Trying to change the external environment won't do any good.

Some people think the remedy for suffering lies outside of them, with God or with Buddha. But that's not the case. The Buddha himself said to his disciples, "I have shown you the path to freedom. Following that path depends on you."

The mind, when used positively—to generate compassion, for example—can create great benefit. It may appear that this benefit comes from God or Buddha, but it is simply the result of the seeds we've planted. And although from the Buddha's teachings we receive the key of knowledge that allows us to change, tame, and train the mind, only we can unlock its deeper truth, exposing our buddha nature with its limitless capacities.

Our current experience is one of relative good fortune. There are many who suffer far worse than we. Ravaged by the relentless pain of war, sickness, or famine, they see no way to change their situations, no way to escape.

If we contemplate their predicament, compassion arises in our hearts. We become inspired not to waste our fortunate circumstances, but to use them to create benefit for ourselves and others, benefit beyond the temporary happiness that comes and goes in the endless cycles of samsaric suffering. Only by fully revealing mind's true nature—by attaining enlightenment—can we find an abiding happiness and help others to do the same. This is the goal of the spiritual path.

2

Working with
Attachment and Desire

TO UNDERSTAND HOW suffering arises, practice watching your mind. Begin by simply letting it relax. Without thinking of the past or the future, without feeling hope or fear about this or that, let it rest comfortably, open and natural. In this space of the mind, there is no problem, no suffering. Then something catches your attention—an image, a sound, a smell. Your mind splits into inner and outer, self and other, subject and object. In simply perceiving the object, there is still no problem. But when you zero in on it, you notice that it's large or small, white or black, square or circular. Then you make a judgment—deciding for example, that it's pretty or ugly—and you react: you like it or you don't.

The problem starts here, because "I like it" leads to "I want it." Similarly, "I don't like it" leads to "I don't want it." If we like something, want it, and can't have it, we suffer. If we want something, get it, and then lose it, we suffer. If we don't want it but can't keep it away, again we suffer. Our suffering seems to stem from the object of our desire or aversion, but that's not so. We suffer because the mind splits into object and subject and becomes involved in wanting or not wanting something.

We often think the only way to create happiness is to try to control the outer circumstances of our lives, to try to fix what seems wrong or to get rid of everything that bothers us. But the real problem lies in our reaction to those circumstances.

There was once a family of shepherds living in Tibet. On a bitterly cold winter day, it was the son's turn to look after the sheep, so his family saved him the largest and best piece of meat for dinner. Upon his return, he looked at the food and burst into tears. When asked what was wrong, he cried, "Why am I always given the worst and smallest portion?"

We have to change the mind and the way we experience reality. Our emotions propel us through extremes, from elation to depression, from good experiences to bad, from happiness to sadness—a constant swinging back and forth. All of this is the by-product of hope and fear, attachment and aversion. We have hope because we are attached to something we want. We have fear because we are averse to something we don't want. As we follow our emotions, reacting to our experiences, we create karma—a perpetual motion that inevitably determines our future. We need to stop the extreme swings of the emotional pendulum so that we can find a place of equilibrium.

When we begin to work with the emotions, we apply the principle of iron cutting iron or diamond cutting diamond. We use thought to change thought. A loving thought can antidote an angry one; contemplation of impermanence can antidote desire.

In the case of attachment, begin by examining what you are attached to. You might think that becoming famous will make you happy. But your fame could trigger jealousy in someone, who might try to kill you. What you worked so hard to create could become the cause of greater suffering. Or you might work diligently to become wealthy, thinking this will bring happiness, only to lose all your money. The source of our suffering is not the loss of wealth in itself, but rather our attachment to having it.

We can lessen attachment by contemplating impermanence. It is certain that whatever we're attached to will either change or be lost. A family member may die or go away, a friend may become an enemy, a thief may steal our money. Even our body, to which we're most attached, will be gone one day. Knowing this not only helps to reduce our attachment, but gives us a greater appreciation of what we have while we have it. There is nothing wrong with money in itself, but if we're attached to it, we'll suffer when we lose it. Instead, we can appreciate it while it lasts, enjoy it, and share it with others without forgetting that it is impermanent. Then if we lose it, the emotional pendulum won't swing as far toward sadness.

Imagine two people who buy the same kind of watch on the same day at the same shop. The first person thinks, "This is a very nice watch. It will be helpful to me, but it may not last long." The second person thinks, "This is the best watch I've ever had. No matter what happens, I can't lose it or let it break." If both people lose their watches, the one who is more attached will be more upset than the other.

If we are fooled by our experience and invest great value in one thing or another, we may find ourselves fighting for what we want and against any opposition. We may think that what we're fighting for is lasting, true, and real, but it's not. It is impermanent, it's neither true nor lasting, and ultimately it's not even real.

We can compare our life to an afternoon at a shopping center. We walk through the shops, led by our desires, taking things off the shelves and tossing them in our baskets. We wander around looking at everything, wanting and longing. We smile at a person or two and continue on, never to see them again.

Driven by desire, we fail to appreciate the preciousness of what we already have. We need to realize that this time with our loved ones, our family, our friends, and our co-workers is very brief. Even if we lived to be a hundred and fifty, we would have very little time to enjoy and make the most of our human opportunity.

Young people think their lives will be long; old people think theirs will end soon. But we can't assume these things. Life comes with a built-in expiration date. There are many strong and healthy people who die young, while many of the old, sick, and feeble live on and on. Not knowing when we'll die, we need to develop an appreciation for and acceptance of what we have rather than continuing to find fault with our experience and incessantly seeking to fulfill our desires.

If we start to worry whether our nose is too big or too small, we should think, "What if I had no head? Now that would be a problem!" As long as we have life, we should rejoice. Although everything may not go exactly as we'd like, we can accept this. If we contemplate impermanence deeply, patience and compassion will arise. We will hold less to the apparent truth of our experience, and the mind will become more flexible. Realizing that one day this body will be buried or cremated, we will rejoice in every moment we have rather than make ourselves or others unhappy.

Now we are afflicted with "me-my-mine-itis," a condition caused by ignorance. Our self-centeredness and self-interest have become very strong habits. In order to change them, we need to refocus. Instead of always concerning ourselves with "I," we must direct our attention to "you," "them," or "others." Reducing self-importance lessens the attachment that stems from it. When we focus beyond ourselves, ultimately we realize the equality of ourselves and all other beings. Everybody wants happiness; nobody wants to suffer. Our attachment to our own happiness expands to encompass attachment to the happiness of all.

Until now, our desires have tended to be transient, superficial, and selfish. If we are going to wish for something, let it be nothing less than complete enlightenment for all beings. That is something worthy of desire. Continually reminding ourselves of what has true worth is an important element of spiritual practice.

Desire and attachment won't disappear overnight. But desire becomes less ordinary when we replace our worldly yearning with the aspiration to do everything we can to help all beings find unchanging happiness. We don't have to abandon the ordinary objects of our desire—relationships, wealth, success—but as we contemplate their impermanence, we become less attached to them. We begin to develop spiritual qualities by rejoicing in our good fortune while recognizing that it won't last.

As attachment arises and disturbs the mind, we can ask, "Why do I feel attachment? Is it of any benefit to myself or others? Is this object of my attachment permanent or lasting?" Through this process, our desires begin to diminish. We commit fewer of the harmful actions that result from attachment, and so create less negative karma. We generate more fortunate karma, and mind's positive qualities gradually increase.

Eventually, as our meditation practice matures, we can try something different from contemplation, from using thought to change thought. We can use an approach that reveals the deeper nature of the emotions as they arise. If you are in the midst of a desire attack—something has captured your mind and you must have it—you won't get rid of the desire by trying to repress it. Instead, you can begin to see through desire by examining it. When it arises, ask yourself, "Where does it come from? Where does it dwell? Can it be described? Does it have any color, shape, or form? When it disappears, where does it go?"

You can say that desire exists, but if you search for the experience, you can't quite grasp it. On the other hand, if you say that it doesn't exist, you're denying the obvious fact that you feel desire. You can't say that it exists, nor can you say that it does not exist. You can't say that it both does and does not exist, or that it neither exists nor does not *not* exist. This is the meaning of the true nature of desire beyond the extremes of conceptual mind.

Our failure to understand the essential nature of an emotion as it arises gets us into trouble. Once we can simply look clearly at what is taking place, neither repressing nor engaging the emotion, it tends to dissolve. If we set a cloudy glass of water aside for a while, it will settle by itself and become clear. Instead of judging the experience of desire, we "liberate it in its own ground" by looking directly at its nature.

Each negative emotion, or mental poison, has an inherent purity that we don't recognize because we are so accustomed to its appearance as emotion. The true nature of the five poisons is the five wisdoms: pride as the wisdom of equanimity; jealousy as all-accomplishing wisdom; attachment and desire as discriminating wisdom; anger and aversion as mirror-like wisdom; and ignorance as the wisdom of the basic space of phenomena. Just as poison can be taken medicinally to effect a cure, each poison of the mind, worked with properly, can resolve into its wisdom nature and thus enhance our spiritual practice.

If while in the throes of desire, you simply relax without moving your attention, you may have a glimpse of discriminating wisdom. Without abandoning desire, you can reveal its wisdom nature.

QUESTION: I'm not sure I understand what you mean by "liberating an emotion in its own ground."

RESPONSE: When an emotion arises, our habit is to become involved in analyzing and reacting to the apparent cause, the outer object. If instead we simply "peel open" the emotion—without attachment or aversion, hatred or involvement—we will reveal and experience its wisdom nature. When we are feeling puffed up and on top of the world, instead of either indulging in our pride or pushing it away, we relax the mind and reveal the essential nature of pride as the wisdom of equanimity.

In working with the emotions, we can apply different methods. When our mind is steeped in duality, in subject–object perception, we cut iron with iron: we antidote a negative thought with a positive one, attachment to our own happiness with attachment to the happiness of others. If we are able to relax the dualistic habit of the mind, we can experience the true essence, or "ground," of an emotion and thus "liberate it in its own ground." In this way, its wisdom principle is revealed.

QUESTION: Can you say more about how contemplating impermanence reduces attachment?

RESPONSE: Imagine a child and an adult on the beach building a sand castle. The adult doesn't think of the sand castle as permanent or real, and isn't attached to it. If a wave washes it away or some children come along and kick it down, the adult doesn't suffer. But the child has begun to think of it as a real castle that will last forever, and so suffers when it's gone.

Similarly, because we have believed for so long that our experience is stable and reliable, we have great attachment to it and suffer when it changes. If we maintain an awareness of impermanence, then we are never completely fooled by the phenomena of samsara.

It is helpful to contemplate the fact that you don't have long to live. Think to yourself, "In the time that I have left, why act on this anger or attachment, which will only produce more confusion and delusion? In taking so seriously what is impermanent and trying to grasp or push it away, I am imagining as solid something that really isn't. I'm only further complicating and perpetuating the delusions of samsara. I won't do that! I'll use this attachment or this aversion, this pride or this jealousy, as practice." Spiritual practice doesn't mean just sitting on a meditation cushion. When you're there with the experience of desire or anger, right there where the mind is active, that is where you practice, at each moment, each step of your life.

QUESTION: In contemplating impermanence, I find my attachment lessening to a certain extent, but wonder how far I should go in dropping things.

RESPONSE: You need to be discriminating in what you address first. Eventually you may drop everything, but begin by abandoning the mind's poisons—for example, anger. Instead of thinking, "Why wash these dishes, they're impermanent?" let go of your anger at having to do them. Also, understand that

whatever arises in the mind, sparking your anger, is impermanent. The anger itself is impermanent. If someone's words upset
you, remember that they are only words, only sounds, not something lasting.

The next thing to drop is attachment to having your own
way. When you understand impermanence, it doesn't matter so
much if things are going as you think they should. If they are,
it's all right. If not, that's all right, too. When you practice like
this, your mind will slowly develop more balance. It won't flip
one way or the other according to whether or not you get what
you want.

QUESTION: Is there anything wrong with being happy or sad,
with feeling our emotions?

RESPONSE: Reminding ourselves when we experience happiness that it's impermanent, that it will eventually disappear, will
help us to cherish and enjoy it while it lasts. At the same time, we
won't become so attached to or fixated on it, and we won't experience so much pain when it's gone.

In the same way, when we experience pain, sorrow, or loss,
we should remind ourselves that these things, too, are impermanent; this will alleviate our suffering. So what keeps us balanced
is an ongoing awareness of impermanence.

QUESTION: Is the self still involved as we expand the focus of
our attachment to the needs of others?

RESPONSE: If you were bound with ropes tied in many knots,
to become free you would have to release the knots, one by one,
in the opposite order in which they were tied. First you'd release

the last knot, then the second to the last, and so forth, until you undid the first, the one closest to you.

We are bound by many knots, including many kinds of attachment. Ideally we would have no clinging at all, but since that is not the case, we use attachment to cut attachment. We begin by untying the last knot: by replacing attachment to our own needs and desires with attachment to the happiness of others.

We need to understand that sooner or later selfish attachment will create problems. If you are attached to your own needs and desires—if you like to be happy and don't like to suffer—when something minor goes wrong, it will seem gigantic. You will focus on it from morning to night, exacerbating the problem. After examination under the microscope of your constant attention, a crack in a teacup will begin to seem like the Grand Canyon.

This self-focusing is itself a kind of meditation. Meditation means bringing something back to the mind again and again. Repeating virtuous thoughts and resting in mind's nature can lead to enlightenment. But self-centered meditation will only produce endless suffering. Focusing on our problems may even lead to suicide—we can become so preoccupied with our own suffering that life seems unbearable and without purpose. Suicide is the worst of solutions because such extreme attachment to death and aversion to human life can close the door to future human rebirth.

So we begin by reducing our self-focus and self-centered thoughts. To do so, we remind ourselves that we aren't the only ones who want to be happy—all beings do. Though others seek happiness, they may not understand how to go about finding it, whereas if we have some understanding of the spiritual path, we can perhaps help and support them in their efforts.

We remind ourselves that of course we'll encounter problems. We're human. But when difficulties arise, we mustn't give them any power. Everyone has problems, many far worse than our own. As we contemplate this, our view expands to include the suffering of others. As our compassion deepens, our relentless self-focusing is reduced; we become more intent on helping others and better able to do so.

If we are sick, it's useful to be attached to the medicine that will make us well. However, once we're cured, that attachment needs to be cut. Otherwise, the very medicine that cured us could make us sick again. We use attachment to benefiting others like medicine in order to cut our self-attachment: we use attachment to change attachment. Eventually, to attain enlightenment, we must cut attachment itself.

QUESTION: How do we change our habit of dwelling on past experiences?

RESPONSE: No experience lasts very long. But we sustain it with our concepts and emotions; we hold on to it, turning it over and over in our mind. Whenever this happens, we need to change the direction of our thoughts. If we find ourselves dwelling on the fact that someone once harmed us, we turn the mind toward compassion and think, "He may have hurt me, but lost in the projections of his confused and deluded mind, he actually hurt rather than helped himself, working at cross-purposes to his desire for happiness."

We also turn the mind toward impermanence. Though someone may have praised or blamed us for something, her words were only like an echo. Like everything else, words simply come and go. Acknowledging their impermanence, we invest them with less solidity and let them go more easily.

In this way we change the habit of fixating on past experiences. It's not enough to redirect the mind only once or twice. We have to do it hundreds of times. Whatever power we give to thoughts of the past, we need to give twice as much to the antidote.

3

Working with
Anger and Aversion

ATTACHMENT AND ANGER are two sides of the same coin. Because of ignorance and the mind's split into subject–object duality, we grasp at or push away what we perceive as external to us. When we encounter something we want and can't have, or someone prevents us from achieving what we've told ourselves we must achieve, or something happens that conflicts with the way we want things to be, we experience anger, aversion, or hatred. But these responses are of no benefit. They only cause harm. Through anger, attachment, and ignorance, the three poisons of the mind, we generate endless karma, endless suffering.

It is said that there is no evil like anger: by its very nature, anger is destructive, an enemy. Because not a shred of happiness ever comes from it, anger is one of the most potent negative forces.

Anger and aversion can lead to aggression. When harmed, many people feel they should retaliate. It's a natural response. "If someone speaks harshly to me, I'll speak harshly in return. If someone hits me, I'll hit him back. That's what he deserves." Or, more extreme: "This person is my enemy. If I kill him, I'll be happy!"

We don't realize that if we have a tendency toward aversion and aggression, enemies start appearing everywhere. We find less and less to like about others, and more and more to hate.

People begin to avoid us, and we become more isolated and lonely. Enraged, we might spit out rough, abusive language. The Tibetans have a saying: "Words may not carry weapons, but they wound the heart." Our words can be extremely harmful, because they not only damage others but evoke their anger. Often a cycle develops: one person feels aversion toward another and says something hurtful; then the other reacts by saying something more cutting. The two fuel each other until they're waging a battle of angry words. This can be extended to national and international levels, where groups of people get caught up in aggression toward other groups, and nations are pitted against nations.

When you give in to aversion and anger, it is as though having decided to kill someone by throwing him into a river, you wrap your arms around his neck, jump into the water, and drown with him. In destroying your enemy, you destroy yourself as well.

It is far better to defuse anger by responding to it with patience, before it can lead to further conflict. Accepting responsibility for what happens to us helps make this possible. We might treat our connection with a perceived enemy as if it came out of nowhere, but in some previous existence we may have spoken harshly to that person, physically abused or harbored angry thoughts about her.

Instead of finding fault with others, directing anger and aversion at situations and people we think are threatening us, we should address the true enemy. That enemy, which destroys our short-term happiness and prevents us in the long term from attaining enlightenment, is our own anger and aversion. If we can vanquish that, there will be no more fights, for we will no longer perceive as enemies those we have been confronting—a great return for a little bit of effort. We, as well as they, will be increasingly less likely to find ourselves repeatedly in situations where conflict could develop. Everyone will benefit.

Our tendency is to contemplate in counterproductive ways. When someone insults us, we usually dwell on it, asking ourselves, "Why did he say that to me? How dare he?" and on and on. It's as if someone shoots an arrow at us, but it falls short. Focusing on the problem is like picking up the arrow and repeatedly stabbing ourselves with it, saying, "He hurt me so much. I can't believe he did that."

Instead, we can use the method of contemplation to think things through differently, to change our habit of reacting with anger. Since it is difficult to think clearly in the midst of an altercation, we begin by practicing at home, alone, imagining confrontations and new ways of responding. Imagine that someone insults you. He's disgusted with you, slaps you, or offends you in some way. You think, "What should I do? I'll defend myself— I'll retaliate. I'll throw him out of my house." Now try another approach. Say to yourself, "This person makes me angry. But what is anger? It is one of the poisons of the mind that creates negative karma, leading to intense suffering. Meeting anger with anger is like following a lunatic who jumps off a cliff. Do I have to do likewise? While it's crazy for him to act the way he does, it's even crazier for me to do the same."

Remember that those who act aggressively toward you are only buying their own suffering, worsening their predicament through ignorance. They think they are doing what is best for themselves, righting a wrong or preventing something worse from happening. But the truth is that their behavior will be of no benefit. They are like someone with a headache beating her head with a hammer to try to stop the pain. In their unhappiness they blame others, who in turn become angry and fight, only making matters worse. When we consider their predicament, we realize that they should be the object of our compassion instead of our blame and anger. Then we aspire to do what we can to protect them from further suffering, as we would a child who keeps misbehaving, running again and again into the road, hitting and scratching us as we attempt to bring her back. Instead of giving up on those who cause harm, we need to realize that they are seeking happiness but don't know how to find it.

The role of enemy isn't a permanent one. The person hurting you now might be your best friend later. Your enemy now could even, in a former lifetime, have been the mother who gave birth to you, fed and took care of you. By contemplating again and again in this way, we learn to respond to aggression with compassion and answer anger with kindness.

Another approach is to develop awareness of the illusory quality of both anger and its object. If someone says to you, "You're a bad person," ask yourself, "Does that make me bad? If I were a bad person and someone said I was good, would that make me good?" If someone says coal is gold, does it become gold? If someone says gold is coal, does it become coal? Things don't change just because someone says this or that. Why take such talk so seriously?

Sit in front of a mirror, look at your reflection, and insult it: "You're ugly. You're bad." Then praise it: "You're beautiful. You're good." Regardless of what you say, the image remains as it is. Praise and blame are not real in and of themselves. Like an echo, a shadow, a mere reflection, they hold no power to help or harm us.

As we practice in this way, we begin to realize that things lack solidity, like dreams or illusions. We develop a more spacious state of mind—one that isn't so reactive. Then when anger arises, instead of responding immediately, we can look at it and ask, "What is this? What is making me turn red and shake? Where is it?" What we discover is that there is no substance to anger, no *thing* to find.

Once we realize we can't find anger, we can let the mind be. We don't repress the anger, push it away, or engage it. We simply let the mind rest in the midst of it. We can stay with the energy itself—simply, naturally, remaining aware of it, without attachment, without aversion. Then we discover that anger, like desire, isn't really what we thought it was. We begin to see its essential nature, mirror-like wisdom.

This may sound easy to do, but it's not. Anger stimulates us and we fly—one way or another. We fly in our mind, we fly off to a judgment or a reaction, becoming involved with whatever has upset us. Our habit of lashing back has been reinforced again and again, lifetime after lifetime. If our understanding of the essence of anger is superficial, we'll find out that we aren't capable of applying it to real-life situations.

There is a well-known Tibetan folk tale of a man meditating in retreat. Somebody came to see him and asked, "What are you meditating on?"

"Patience," he said.

"You're a fool!"

This made the meditator furious and he began to argue with his visitor—which proved exactly how much patience he had.

Only through scrupulous, methodical application of these methods, day by day, month by month, year by year, will we dissolve our deeply ingrained habits. The process may take some time, but we *will* change. Look how quickly we change in negative ways. We're quite happy, and then somebody says or does something and we get irritated. Changing in positive ways requires discipline, exertion, and patience. The word for "meditation" in Tibetan (*gom*) can also be translated as "to become familiar with." Using a variety of methods, we become familiar with other ways of being.

There is an expression: "Even an elephant can be tamed in various ways." When goads or hooks are used skillfully, this enormous, powerful beast can be led along very gently. It is said that when elephants are decorated for festive occasions, they become docile, moving as though they were walking on eggshells. And in a large crowd of people, they are very easily controlled. So something that is big and ungainly can actually be managed well with the proper means. In the same way, the mind, often unwieldy and wild, can be tamed with skillful methods.

A worldly person approaches life differently than a spiritual practitioner. A worldly person always looks at phenomena as if through a window, judging the outer experience; a practitioner, on the other hand, uses experience as a mirror to examine his own mind repeatedly, in minute detail, to determine where the strengths and weaknesses lie, how to develop the former and eliminate the latter.

We don't need a psychic to predict our future—we need only look at our own mind. If we have a good heart and helpful intentions toward others, we will find happiness. If instead our mind is filled with ordinary self-centered thoughts, or with anger and harmful intentions toward others, we will only meet with difficulties.

If we continuously check the mind, applying antidotes to the poisons as they arise, we will slowly see change. Only we can really know what is taking place in our mind. It is easy to lie to others. We can pretend that a thick leather bag is full, but as soon as someone sits on it, he'll know the truth. Similarly, we can sit for hours in meditation posture, but if poisonous thoughts circulate in the mind all the while, we're only pretending to do spiritual practice. Instead, we can be honest with ourselves, taking responsibility for what we see in our own mind instead of judging others, and apply the appropriate remedy for change.

QUESTION: Is it wrong for me to feel anger toward those responsible for war, for killing so many?

RESPONSE: A killer is as worthy of our compassion as is his victim. The victim's death fulfills a karmic debt. On the other hand, the killer is sowing seeds for future suffering on an enormous scale, far greater than that of his victim, and doesn't even realize it. Surely both the victim and the killer deserve our compassion.

One of our greatest concerns today is the attainment of world peace, an end toward which many groups and individuals struggle with noble intention. However, if aggression is involved and we are *fighting* for peace, if one group says to another, "You're not making peace in the world so we're going to force you to do what we think is better," we are only fueling the anger that gave rise to the conflict in the first place. Instead, we need to develop compassion and helpfulness in all directions.

Our efforts to create world peace will depend on how we as individuals react to situations. If we do so with anger, hatred, aversion, and aggression, we will only exacerbate the problem. So it is important not only to cultivate noble ideals, but to uphold and embody them throughout our lives.

QUESTION: What is the difference between anger and wrath?

RESPONSE: The difference lies in one's motivation. Wrath is based on deep-hearted compassion and selfless motivation. One may act forcefully and may even appear to be angry, but the intention is not to harm or to punish, only to benefit—for example, by protecting someone from the effects of her actions. Anger, on the other hand, is motivated by selfish attachment to what one wants, aversion to what one doesn't want, or the desire to punish or harm someone.

QUESTION: As I continue to do spiritual practice, will my anger just go away?

RESPONSE: At first you will feel as much anger as before, but will be less inclined to act on it. With more practice, you will experience it less frequently. Eventually, a lot farther down the spiritual path, your anger will arise as mirror-like wisdom.

QUESTION: How do we deal with anger in the moment, when it's coming up strongly and we're trying not to act on it?

RESPONSE: If you feel a strong desire for a piece of delicious-looking cake but learn that the cake is laced with poison, your desire for it will vanish. Similarly, when you truly understand that anger is poisonous, your desire to act on it will subside.

QUESTION: Do our endless anger and desire imply that we have "original sin," that our true nature is inherently flawed?

RESPONSE: Absolutely not. If our nature were flawed, spiritual means could not reduce our negativity and bring forth our positive qualities. Because our nature is perfect, we can use methods to remove the superficial obscurations that conceal that pristine purity.

4

Working with Ignorance

IN TRACING THE CAUSES of our confusion and suffering, we come to the fundamental problem of ignorance. The reason that we suffer as we do, that we encounter the problems we do, and that we continue to wander in samsara is that we are unaware of our true nature. This lack of recognition expresses itself in our projection and experience of the phenomenal world, which appears to us as solid, composed of the various elements. We are continually under the impression that there is an "I" poised against everything else that isn't "I." Because of this dualistic tendency of mind, we objectify our experience and make judgments about the objects we perceive. This leads to attachment and aversion, which generate karma and endless suffering. Dualistic clinging, emotional confusion, habit, karma, and the fruits of karma are all consequences of this lack of recognition.

Because we don't know the true nature of our body, speech, or mind, our environment, the past or future, we take daily events to be true—just as when we are dreaming, we take our dreams to be true. When we dream at night, in a sense we're confused because we believe we're actually in a particular place, doing certain things: driving a car, building something, even running from a tiger.

In a dream we remember the past and can anticipate a future. Sky, ground, breathing, swallowing—everything seems real. Actually, we're asleep in bed and nothing is really happening. Yet while we dream, our reality is dream-reality. If a dream-tiger chases us, we run as fast as we can to save our life.

Once we wake up, or become aware in the dream that we're dreaming, our confusion disappears. The tiger has no more power and we're no longer afraid, because we realize that the whole drama was created by our own mind. As long as we're dreaming and remain in the grip of confusion, hope and fear persist; the consequences seem crucial. But when the knowledge that we're dreaming dispels our confusion, we have no more hope or fear.

In actuality, all experience—whether the suffering of samsara or the bliss of nirvana—is as insubstantial as our dreams. All of it is unreal, untrue. It is an unceasing, luminous, magnificent, and illusory display.

Our life from birth to death resembles one long dream, and each dream we have at night is a dream within a dream. Perhaps you've experienced dreaming at night and then waking up and telling somebody, "I had an amazing dream." You make coffee, you're ready to go to work, and suddenly the alarm goes off and you really wake up. You hadn't been awake before at all. You'd only dreamed you were awake. This is called a false awakening, a dream of waking, and it's what we do every morning of our lives. In the dream of life, we think we're awake, but in fact we're still dreaming. It's just that the alarm clock hasn't sounded yet.

We're dreamers and we experience short dreams of the night within this long dream of life, within the even longer dream of samsaric becoming. We've been taught and assume that our daily reality is real and true, so when something difficult happens, we suffer. We've also been taught that our dreams are illusions, so we tend to suffer less from our nightmares than from the events in our daily lives. The dream world comes and goes; it's clearly impermanent, so we think it's not real. Yet the same is true of our daily reality. It, too, is impermanent. The only difference between them is how long each lasts.

To know that our reality is not the whole truth of existence frees us from suffering. We're no longer controlled by our fears or our attachments. Yet the mind easily falls back into its old assumptions with the next movement of this daytime dream. Suddenly a lovely woman or a wonderful man appears, and once again we find ourselves believing in the dream we call reality. We've been fooled again; the illusion hasn't been completely dispelled—it only flickered for a second. We briefly realized the deeper nature of our experience, but the realization didn't hold.

We need a method for remembering that we're only dreaming, for truly breaking through our confusion, not just glimpsing the truth in one moment and forgetting it in the next. We need to clearly and decisively bring our deluded experience of reality to an end. This requires authentic recognition of the truth of our experience. Like the true nature of the night dream, it is beyond the extremes of conceptual thought, of "is" and "is not," and cannot be grasped by the rational mind.

Suppose we discover a large piece of gold but fail to realize its value. Our lack of recognition doesn't lessen its worth, nor would our recognition increase it. It simply is what it is. If we know its value, we will use it appropriately. If we don't, we might use it to hold open a screen door or to prop up a big book.

The foundational nature of the mind is already gold; we simply don't recognize it as such. The goal of the spiritual path is complete realization of the gold; the path is how we accomplish that goal, making obvious what already exists.

In the method of meditation called dream yoga, the first step is to realize while we dream that we are dreaming. The next is to maintain this realization, at which point we acquire a creative capacity in the dream. If you were dreaming of a single balloon and could maintain your understanding of the nature of the dream, you could make many more balloons appear. Or a single person could become many; this world could become a different one. In short, we develop the ability to transform our dreams because the falseness of the dream no longer commands us. In recognizing its nature, we command the dream.

It is exactly the same in our daytime reality, from the moment we're born until we die. Many people have come to realize the true nature of this life's experience. In the Buddhist tradition, they are called *mahasiddhas*. In other traditions as well, people have attained such great realization that ordinary rules of reality failed to bind them. Jesus walked on water; great realized ones can leave footprints in stone or fly through the sky. What is hot to us is not hot to them, what's cold, not cold, nor solid, solid. They command reality; it does not command them.

To know the true nature of our experience, and to maintain that knowing, is the way to attain enlightenment. Enlightenment is not anything new or something we create or bring into existence. It simply means discovering within us what is already there. It is the full realization of our intrinsic nature, our buddha nature. In Tibetan, "buddha" is *sang gyay*. *Sang* means that all faults have been cleared away, while *gyay* connotes full realization. Just as from darkness, the moon waxes, likewise from ignorance, the qualities of mind's nature emerge.

Like water, which is fluid in its natural state but turns to ice when frozen, the true nature of mind—which can be called God, Buddha, perfection—seems to be different when obscured by confusion and delusion. But that nature hasn't gone anywhere, just as the water hasn't gone anywhere. When ice melts, the water regains its natural qualities. When mind's obscurations are removed, our nature becomes apparent.

Bound by our belief in the dream we call life, we can't perceive our true nature. As dreamers, however, we have choices; we can create good or bad life dreams. If we wish to make them good, we must change. Otherwise, the mind, left to its old habits, will not necessarily create better dreams.

We can also choose not to dream at all, but instead to wake up. To awaken fully means to recognize the greater truth—the pure nature of body, speech, and mind. If we want to wake up, however, we won't automatically emerge from our deep sleep. We need methods, and we need to apply them.

Wisdom—knowing our true nature—is the antidote to ignorance—not knowing. It is the lamp that dispels the darkness of our mind. Through the threefold process of listening to, contemplating, and meditating on the teachings, we can eventually bring forth wisdom that goes beyond our everyday, ordinary knowing.

Initially, someone who understands more than we do introduces us to something greater than anything we've ever known. But hearing this teaching, even in detail, isn't enough to engender belief in what we've been told. Blind faith isn't very useful, because only if we understand what we've been taught can we harness all our abilities to our practice.

No matter how clearly we understand what has been said, listening to teachings in itself does not reduce suffering. To do so, we need to assimilate the wisdom that comes through them. We need to think about them, bringing our intellect and intelligence to bear, reflecting, questioning, and examining to see if what we have been taught is true, to see if it works.

In this process of contemplation, questions arise. We search for answers, and then contemplate again. If we don't investigate and probe, if we don't remove doubt, then doing spiritual practice will be like trying to sew with a two-pointed needle. We won't get very far. Through contemplation, we develop a deeper comprehension and certainty beyond intellectual knowledge, the mere amassing of facts.

However, even profound understanding can be forgotten. So we repeatedly apply that understanding to our experience until it becomes more intuitive. Finally, through the process of meditation, our inherent wisdom becomes completely obvious.

QUESTION: Does "waking up" mean that everything we see, hear, and taste will disappear?

RESPONSE: As we awaken to our true nature, the phenomenal world as we know it won't disappear, but our reactions to it will change and our suffering will diminish accordingly. If in the midst of a frightening dream, we suddenly realize we're dreaming, though the dream itself won't necessarily end, our fear will. We are helpless in the face of our hopes and fears, likes and dislikes, overwhelmed by all kinds of things, because we believe them to be true. But if we realize that whatever happens is illusory, it loses validity and so won't have the same power over us. As a result, we won't experience as much suffering.

Rather than getting caught up in our dreamlike experience, be it one of happiness or sadness, we must look beyond what is impermanent, to its essence. To know that essence is called "great knowing"; to know only ordinary reality and the seeming solidity of things is called "ordinary knowing." The difference between them is like the difference between two roads: the road of the dream—that of perpetual suffering—and the great road of realization. Great knowing is the basis for transforming our ordinary experience into the realization of absolute truth.

5

Daily Life as Spiritual Practice

AS A WAY OF INTRODUCING the topic of meditation in daily life, I'd like to draw on some of my own experiences and training in Tibet. There, at the age of two, I was recognized as a *tulku,* one who has directed successive rebirths for the benefit of others. This means that I was expected to turn out rather special. By the age of five, I'd been taught to read and write. I had my own tutor, which in one way was very fortunate, because every day, all day, someone sat in attendance teaching me. On the other hand, whenever I made a mistake or forgot a lesson, I encountered the swing of the stick.

Even as a very young child I found myself exposed to profound spiritual teachings, either in a group or just one-on-one with my tutor. I studied the nature of absolute and relative truth. And it was then that I first received the teaching on impermanence. Once our universe wasn't here. Slowly it came into being, and over time it will age and at some point dissipate. Even our own body wasn't here at one time. Each day it ages and some day it will cease to be. Everything in our experience is subject to impermanence. Recognizing this truth is fundamental to developing a spiritual perspective.

When I was introduced to this teaching, I resisted it strongly; I simply didn't want to hear it. I thought, yes, of course, seasons change, people change, lives change—who cares? I didn't pay a lot of attention to it. But by the age of nine, after having heard the teaching again and again, I'd begun to contemplate impermanence. By then, I had gained a little realization of its nature.

At first, understanding impermanence didn't change things drastically for me. I experienced just a little less grasping, desire, and attachment to the things in life we normally become attached to. The change was subtle, based on the realization that things weren't quite as real as they had previously seemed to be.

That shift in perspective was tremendously helpful at the time my mother died, when I was only eleven years old. It also helped when I was twelve and my brother died, and at thirteen when my very dear guardian and teacher had to leave. Those experiences of death and separation were not easy, but the understanding I had gained from contemplating impermanence made them less unbearable, and helped again later when I had to face the loss of my monastery and country.

I learned that the more attached we are to our possessions and relationships in the world, the more important and necessary we think they are, the more pain we experience when they cease to be. For this reason alone, it is crucial to contemplate impermanence.

It is also very important to understand the good fortune of having a human body. Most of us take human existence lightly, too much for granted; we become callous to the natural joy of having a human form. We may not all have the eye of wisdom, but those who do describe realms of experience other than our own. Still, the greatest opportunity of all is that of a human birth. In another realm we might enjoy a body that is seemingly superior, but we will never be able to accomplish what we can as a human. We simply won't have the capability.

Sometimes people fail to realize the incomparable opportunity they have, because their lives are disappointing or very trying, and they lose interest in taking advantage of their human capacities. That is a grave mistake. The potential this body provides, right now, is far too great to be overlooked because of disappointment or difficulty.

It's as if you borrow a boat to cross a river, and instead of using it right away, you take your time, forgetting that it isn't yours but has only been lent to you. If you don't take advantage of it while you have it, you'll never get across the river, for sooner or later the boat will be reclaimed, the opportunity lost.

This human body is a rare vehicle, and we need to use it well without delay. The most exalted purpose of a precious human birth is to advance spiritually. If we are not able to travel far, still we can make some progress; even better, we can help others to progress. At the very least, we mustn't make other people miserable.

Life is like a Sunday afternoon picnic—it doesn't last very long. Just to look at the sun, to smell the flowers, to breathe the fresh air is a joy. But if all we do is fight about where to put the blanket, who's going to sit on which corner, who gets the wing or the drumstick—what a waste! Sooner or later, rain clouds come, dark approaches, and the picnic is over. And all we've done is bicker. Think of what we've lost.

You might wonder: if everything is impermanent and nothing lasts, how can anyone live happily? It's true that we can't really hold on to things, but we can use that realization to look at life differently, as a very brief and precious opportunity. If we bring to our lives the knowledge that everything is impermanent, our experiences will become richer, our relationships more sincere, and our appreciation greater for what we already enjoy.

We will also be more patient. We'll realize that no matter how bad things might seem now, such unfortunate circumstances cannot last. We'll feel we can endure them until they pass. And with greater patience, we'll be gentler with those around us. It's not so hard to extend a loving gesture once we realize that we may never see a great aunt again. Why not make her happy? Why not take the time to listen to all those old stories?

Coming to an understanding of impermanence and a genuine desire to make others happy in this brief time we have together represents the beginning of true spiritual practice. It is this kind of sincerity that truly catalyzes transformation. We don't have to shave our heads or wear special robes. We don't have to leave home or sleep on a bed of stone. Spiritual practice doesn't require austere conditions, only a good heart and an understanding of impermanence. This will lead to progress.

If we only make a show of spirituality—burning the right incense, sitting the right way, speaking the right words—we're liable to become prouder, more self-righteous, condescending, and faultfinding. Such false practice won't help us or others at all. The purpose of spiritual practice is to reduce our faults, not to increase them.

Having heard this once, we may become inspired. It makes us happy to hear such truths. But it's a bit like patching a hole in a piece of clothing: if we don't sew the patch on well, pretty soon it will start to slip and the hole will show again.

This brings us to contemplation and meditation. Although we may be inspired and touched by the simplicity and profundity of a spiritual approach to life, our habits are very strong and our difficulties in the world remain. Effective practice requires constant reiteration of what we know to be true.

Meditation is like the process of stitching, of reminding ourselves again and again of the deeper truths—impermanence, loving kindness—until the patch is sewn on so strongly that it becomes a part of the cloth and strengthens the whole garment. Then we're not shaken by outer circumstances. There is a kind of ease that comes when we understand the illusory nature of reality, when we comprehend the dreamlike quality of life, the impermanence that pervades everything. This doesn't mean that we deny our involvement with life. Rather, we don't take it quite so seriously; we approach it with less hope and fear. Then we're like the adult playing with a child on the beach: we don't suffer as the child does if the sand castle is washed away, yet compassion arises in us for others' suffering.

Compassion is natural to every one of us, but because we have deep-seated, self-centered habits, we need to cultivate it by contemplating the suffering of those who invest their dream with solidity. We need to develop a sincere, compassionate desire that their suffering will cease, that they will come to understand the dreamlike quality of life and thus avoid agony over the inevitable loss of things they value.

For twelve years a great Indian scholar and practitioner, Atisha, studied many texts—huge bodies of teachings and commentaries on the doctrine of the Buddha and the realization of great lamas. After his years of study, he came to the conclusion that all of the 84,000 methods that the Buddha taught for achieving the transition from ordinary to extraordinary mind came down to the essential point of good heart.

When we merely talk about purity of heart, it seems simple enough, but in difficult times we find that it is not so easy to maintain. If we are face-to-face with someone who hates us and would hurt us, it is very hard not to become angry and lose our loving kindness.

An effective way to uphold good heart in our daily interactions is to repeatedly remind ourselves that every being has, at some time in our many lifetimes, been our parent. This may prove difficult for some of us to accept. But the Buddha and other beings with omniscience and infallible wisdom have taught that we have all had countless lifetimes. We, on the other hand, don't know where we were before we were born or what will happen to us after we die. If we think about it, though, we live today as a consequence of having lived yesterday, and today supplies the basis for tomorrow. The sequence of existence is similar. We have this life, which means there was some previous basis for it, while the present itself forms the ground for what will occur next.

If our inherent wisdom were more fully revealed, we would see that all beings—human, animal, or otherwise—at some time throughout countless lifetimes have shown us the kindness of parents: given us a body, protected us, enabled us to survive, provided education, understanding, and some sort of worldly training. It doesn't matter what their roles are now or how difficult our relationships with them may be. It's as if we are playing at make-believe. We're like actors who have come to believe we're actually the characters we're portraying.

When we truly understand our connection with every other being, equanimity arises. We regard everyone, friend or foe, with consideration. Even though someone may prove difficult, that doesn't mean she hasn't been important to us before.

When we see one who was once our parent suffering terribly, our compassion deepens. We think, "How sad—she doesn't understand. If I understand a little bit more, it's my responsibility to help her as much as I can."

A perception like that softens us. So when we're in a stressful situation, before we react impulsively, we think for a moment, then respond with patience and compassion instead of anger. We try to be kind and helpful, and refrain from hurtful, self-interested, negative actions and faultfinding.

Spiritual practice in daily life begins when you wake up in the morning. Rejoice that you didn't die in the night, knowing you have one more useful day—you can't guarantee that you'll have two. Then remind yourself of correct motivation. Instead of setting out to become rich and famous or to follow your own selfish interests, meet the day with an altruistic intention to help others. And renew your commitment every morning. Tell yourself, "Today I'll do the best that I can. In the past I've done fairly well on some days, terribly on others. But since this day may be my last, I will offer my best; I will do right by other people as much as I am able."

When you go to bed at night, don't just hit the pillow and pass out. Instead, review the day. Ask yourself, "How did I do? It was my intention not to hurt anybody—did I accomplish that? I meant to cultivate joy, compassion, love, equanimity—did I do so?" Think not just of this day, but of your life as a whole. "Have I developed positive tendencies? Have I basically been a virtuous person? Or have I spent most of my time acting negatively, engaged in nonvirtuous activities?" Consider these things critically and honestly. How does it come out when you really study the tallies?

If you find that you have fallen short, there is no benefit in feeling guilty or blaming yourself. The point is to observe what you have done, because your harmful actions can be purified. Negativity is not indelibly marked in the ground of the mind. It can be changed. So look back; when you see your faults and downfalls, call upon a wisdom being. You don't need to go anywhere special, for there is no place where prayer is not heard. It doesn't matter whether you pray to God, Buddha, or a deity, as long as the object of your supplication is flawless and without limitation. From absolute perfection you receive the blessings of purification.

With a wisdom being as your witness, confess with sincere regret the harm you've done, vowing not to repeat it. As you meditate, visualize light radiating from that being, cleansing you and purifying all the mistakes of your day, your life, every life you've lived.

When you look back on the day, you may find that you were able to make others happy. You may have given food to a hungry animal or practiced generosity and patience. Rather than becoming self-satisfied, resolve to do even better tomorrow, to be more skillful, more compassionate in your interactions with others. Dedicate the positive energy created by your actions to all beings, whoever they are, whatever condition they're in, thinking, "May this virtue relieve the suffering of beings; may it cause them short- and long-term happiness."

During the day, check your mind. How am I behaving? What is my real intention? You can't really know anybody else's mind; the only one you truly know is your own. Whenever you can, contemplate the preciousness of human birth, impermanence, karma, and the suffering of others.

In daily meditation practice, we work with two aspects of the mind: its intellectual ability to reason and conceptualize, and the quality that is beyond thought—the pervasive, nonconceptual nature of mind. Using the rational faculty, contemplate; then let the mind rest. Think and then relax; contemplate, then relax. Don't use one or the other exclusively, but both together, like the two wings of a bird.

This isn't just something you do while sitting on a cushion. You can meditate this way anywhere—while driving your car or while working. It doesn't require special props or a special environment. It can be practiced in every situation.

Some people think that if they meditate for fifteen minutes a day, they ought to become enlightened in a week and a half. But it doesn't work like that. Even if you meditate, pray, and contemplate for an hour each day, that's one hour you're meditating and twenty-three you're not. What are the chances of one person against twenty-three in a tug-of-war? It isn't possible to change the mind with one hour of daily meditation. You have to pay attention to your spiritual process throughout the day, as you work, play, sleep; the mind always has to be moving toward the ultimate goal of enlightenment.

When you are out and about in the world, stay focused on what you are doing. If you are writing, keep your mind on the stroke of the pen. If you are sewing, focus on the stitch. Don't get distracted. Don't think of a hundred things at the same time. Don't get going on what happened yesterday or what might happen in the future. It doesn't matter what you are doing as long as you focus the mind one-pointedly. Hold to your task closely, comfortable in what you do, and in that way you will train your mind.

Always check yourself thoroughly: reduce negative thoughts, words, and actions, increase those that are positive, and continually bring your mind back to what you are doing. Meditation involves a constant refocusing. You have to bring pure intention back again and again. Then relax the mind to allow a direct, subtle recognition of that which lies beyond all thought.

If you have a hard time remembering to practice throughout the day, find a method to remind yourself, in the same way that someone might put a string around her finger. You could tell yourself that whenever you walk outside you will give rise to compassion, or that every time you start the car you will pray. In Tibet there was a great lama who devised an effective, if unconventional, reminder for his mother, who had created a lot of nonvirtue in her life. He taught her the mantra *Om Mani Padme Hung* and encouraged her to recite it as much as possible. Unfortunately, she didn't show much enthusiasm for mantra repetition, so the lama placed a small bell on her spinning wheel and another in the kitchen, instructing her to recite *Om Mani Padme Hung* whenever she heard one of them ring. As the old woman spun her wool and went about her work in the kitchen, the bells rang. She loved her son, but she didn't love the dharma. So every time she heard them, she would sing, "This is my penalty! *Om Mani Padme Hung*. This is the law! *Om Mani Padme Hung*. This is my son's command! *Om Mani Padme Hung*." Although her motivation was less than flawless, these constant reminders encouraged her practice of virtue.

There are, of course, established centers where you can hear the Buddha's teachings, where you are exposed to a different view of reality and can meditate and contemplate in a supportive environment. It's hard to make progress on your own and to change if you hear the teachings only once. It's very helpful to visit such centers, but whether you do or not, you need to integrate what you have learned with a care that requires constant attention, listening to and applying the teachings again and again.

It doesn't happen swiftly, but the mind can change. There was once a man who decided to keep track of his thoughts. This isn't an easy process, for though one can be determined to watch one's thoughts, many get away, coming and going without being noticed. Nevertheless, he put down a white stone for every virtuous thought, a black stone for every nonvirtuous one. At first this produced a huge pile of black stones, but as the years went by, the pile of black stones slowly became smaller while the white pile grew. That's the kind of gradual progress we make with sincere effort. There is nothing flashy about the progress of the mind; it's very measured and steady, requiring diligence, attentiveness, patience, and enthusiastic perseverance.

There are many profound teachings in the Buddhist tradition, but what we've been discussing is the essential, sweet nectar of them all. Cultivating good heart in every aspect of daily life, practicing virtue, compassion, equanimity, love, and joy—this is the way to enlightenment.

QUESTION: You have taught that the difference between practitioners and nonpractitioners is that nonpractitioners perceive the phenomenal world as if looking through a window, whereas practitioners do so as if looking in a mirror. Could you say more about this, since it is so important for our practice?

RESPONSE: If we want to help others eliminate flaws and develop positive qualities, we have to ensure that we ourselves have at least purified our own mind enough to benefit others rather than simply criticize them. We need to focus on our own flaws rather than on others'. When we have a negative thought, or even a neutral one, we must try to transform it into a virtuous one. The more we redirect the mind toward virtue the more its outer expression in speech and actions will become virtuous. This will create karma that leads to happiness instead of suffering.

If we repeatedly examine our thoughts, words, and actions and tame our own mind, our shortcomings will begin to diminish and our positive qualities will increase. The more we reduce our flaws, the more those around us will benefit. The more we enhance our positive qualities, the more we will be capable of helping others do so. As we practice in this way, we will begin to see differences in our relationships. We may find ourselves becoming more patient, loving, and kind, less likely to get into arguments, more inclined to find peaceful resolutions to conflict. Close relationships often provide the greatest test of patience. Our interactions with larger groups, at work or in our neighborhood, will also show us how well our practice is working.

QUESTION: How can I bring spirituality into my daily life without neglecting my responsibilities?

RESPONSE: Following the spiritual path doesn't mean neglecting things that need attention. You must continue to earn a living, maintain a home, and feed yourself and your family. But broaden your motivation. Understand that if you eat well and stay healthy, you may live longer, affording more time for practice so that you can increase your ability to benefit others. Expand your commitment to act on behalf of all beings, not just your family and friends.

We needn't abandon worldly life, yet we must understand its illusory nature. Even as you earn money to support your family, don't be fooled by the seeming reality of the experience. Remember impermanence. Awareness of the play of change imparts a stability to the mind, an equanimity not disrupted by loss or tragedy. We don't have to give up working toward goals, and it's wonderful when we achieve them. But if we can't, we won't become upset, because we never believed they were that important to begin with.

When we die, we'll lose everything anyway. In the meantime, life is like a dance. Phenomena arise and subside; thoughts and emotions arise and subside. Trying neither to stop nor to engage them, we simply observe the illusory quality of the dance.

PART II

*The Four Thoughts That
Turn the Mind*

6

The Importance of the
Four Thoughts

FROM THE BIOGRAPHIES of great practitioners, we see that exemplary saints and masters were unflagging in their pursuit of the spiritual path. They were willing to put up with all manner of challenges and hardships, practicing day and night with inspiration and enthusiasm, because of their profound understanding and assimilation of what are known in Buddhism as "the four thoughts that turn the mind toward dharma."

Contemplating the four thoughts upholds our practice, just as a foundation supports a building. In constructing a home, if we arrange the foundational stones so that they hold firmly and don't shift, we can build a fine structure, one we can live in for a very long time. Instead, if we take whatever comes to hand and throw something up overnight, we won't end up with anything useful. Sooner or later the whole building will come tumbling down.

Similarly, if we listen to, contemplate, and practice the Buddha's teachings—the dharma—in a superficial way, we may discover after ten or fifteen years that there has been no real change, that we experience the same attachment, ignorance, and aggression as before. Bound by ordinary habits of mind, we find our ability to benefit ourselves and others severely limited. We might be tempted to conclude that there is something wrong with the teachings, that Buddhist methods don't work. But they work just fine; it's the practitioner who isn't making the necessary effort to change.

We must strive from the depth of our heart to develop a firm foundation for our practice. Otherwise, we'll fault the teachings and become discouraged. We'll fabricate all kinds of excuses to avoid practicing; all sorts of outer circumstances and inner obstacles—disease, physical discomfort, mental stress—will seem to stand in the way.

Among the obstacles to our path is the fact that we are dominated by our attachments. We have many needs and desires we feel we absolutely must fulfill. By meditating on two of the four thoughts—first, the freedom and opportunity of our precious human existence and the difficulty of obtaining it, and second, impermanence—we come to realize that our human birth is as rare as our time is short. Contemplating these two thoughts helps to reduce the mind's poisons and steer us toward liberation. Carrying these thoughts with us throughout our daily lives—with our families, at work, or in formal meditation—we develop more equanimity and ease in dealing with life's changes. In reordering our priorities, we develop contentment as well. We come to understand that enough is enough—when we have a hundred of something, we don't need a thousand; when we have ten thousand, we don't need a million. We learn that if we continually try to satisfy ever-increasing worldly demands and desires, we will always remain dissatisfied.

Nonetheless, we may still find ourselves seeking only relative rather than ultimate happiness, thinking only of how to make our worldly circumstances the very best they can be in this and future lives. Because such shortsightedness creates further obstacles to liberation, we meditate on the second two of the four thoughts—the principle of karma, or cause and effect, and the suffering that pervades cyclic existence. By contemplating these two thoughts, we reduce our attachment to conventional happiness and experience a gradual loosening of increasingly subtle ties to samsara.

With less attachment to our worldly experience, we deepen our commitment to the path of enlightenment, removing everything counterproductive, bringing together everything supportive to our goal. This is why the four thoughts are called the preliminaries. If we want a cart to take us somewhere, we must put a horse before that cart.

Many people believe these teachings are for beginners. They want to hurry on to something "profound," beyond what they think of as "kindergarten dharma." But contemplation of the four thoughts is among the most profound and beneficial practices on the path to enlightenment, for they are the foundational truths that underlie the entire spiritual path.

7

The Lama

CONTEMPLATION OF the four thoughts is among the skill-ful methods we use to reduce the mind's poisons and create short- and long-term benefit for ourselves and others. Since we don't have the fortune to have learned the methods of liberation directly from the Buddha Shakyamuni, it is the lama, our spiritual teacher, who introduces such teachings to us. Yet before we come to rely on a lama, it is essential that we carefully examine his qualities, just as we would investigate a doctor's qualifications before placing our life in her hands. In a sense, if we didn't investigate a doctor, it wouldn't be such a big deal, because her incompetence might cause us to lose only this one life. But if we place our faith in a spiritual teacher who isn't qualified, we might develop counterproductive habits that could remain with us for lifetimes to come and create tremendous obstacles on the path to enlightenment.

A spiritual teacher must fulfill two requirements: first, that she has listened to, contemplated, and understood the teachings and, second, has meditated upon them and gained realization of their essential meaning. Only someone with recognition of mind's nature can introduce us to that nature and give us methods for breaking through the habitual patterns of attachment and aversion that prevent us from stabilizing that recognition in our own mind. Such a teacher can also help us cultivate the selfless intention to awaken from the dream of life so that we can help others do the same—the sole reason for engaging in the path.

Eloquence is not the most important quality of a lama, for it isn't so difficult to deliver a nice lecture; it is much more important that, through a genuine and profound practice of meditation, the lama maintains a direct, personal experience of the teachings. Otherwise, he might be like a parrot who incessantly repeats, "Practice virtue, don't practice nonvirtue," but devours an insect as soon as it enters its cage.

These days it is difficult to ascertain a lama's qualities. At least one out of every ten or twenty people claims to be a teacher with great scholarly and meditational achievement. No one hangs out a shingle declaring "I am a bad teacher." Ideally one should learn from an outside source how and where a lama studied the dharma and practiced meditation. It is even more important to observe the lama firsthand, to carefully determine whether she is good-hearted and truly lives the teachings. It would be hard to find a completely faultless teacher; even if we did, we wouldn't realize it. Nonetheless, we can rely on a lama who, through meditation, has removed some of the mind's obscurations, attained some degree of realization, and developed great compassion. Lamas with good heart have your interests, not theirs, in mind. If they can't answer a question or help you, they will direct you to someone who can. They won't lead you astray.

It is risky to make too hasty a commitment to a lama. But once you have come to a carefully considered decision, you must follow his teachings diligently and purposefully. If you are sick but don't take the medicine your physician prescribes, you won't get well. So after choosing a lama skillfully, you must listen and train skillfully. If you carefully apply the instructions you have received, then slowly your negativity will decrease, and love and compassion will increase. In this way, you will learn what the lama has learned.

The lama is like a mold that shapes the student's mind. A student won't develop good qualities from a poor teacher, but will benefit without fail by following a good teacher's instructions. This is why we call upon the lama at the beginning of our contemplation of the four thoughts. We remember the lama's qualities and pray that, through her blessings, obstacles to our practice will dissolve, our mind will turn toward the dharma, and the door to liberation will be opened.

8

Precious Human Birth

IMAGINE THAT YOU are very poor and suddenly find yourself in a land where everything is studded with gems, gold, and coins. You live there for many years, but one day must return home, making a perilous journey by sea with no possibility of ever returning to the jeweled land. Once home, you realize that you hadn't thought to bring anything back with you—not a single jewel, not a speck of gold dust. Think how regretful you would be!

In the same way, we move through the cycles of suffering lifetime after lifetime, lacking the merit—the virtue and positive energy—necessary to propel us out of samsara. Then a few rare conditions come together to produce this precious human existence with its immense opportunity. If we die without using it to full advantage, we will have departed from the human realm empty-handed, having accomplished nothing. The first thought that turns the mind toward dharma concerns the preciousness of our human birth and the importance of using it well.

People sometimes wonder, "Why was I born? What is the purpose of my life? I have a feeling there is some great reason for my being here, but I don't know what it is." Some think their purpose is to play music or to write outstanding books. Yet any music performed, anything written, is impermanent.

We don't understand that our mind is the dreamer and our life experience the dream it has made. Because we have no idea that we are dreaming, we take life very seriously and often feel helpless when things don't go as we wish. Through spiritual practice, at the very least we can make happy dreams. Eventually, we can actually wake up.

Waking up, revealing the essence of our existence, is the overriding purpose of our lives. But what is this essence? It can't be our body, since all that is left when the mind leaves the body is a corpse. Nor can it be our speech, since that is simply a function of the body. And it isn't our vacillating emotions, the endless ups and downs brought on by hope and fear, attraction and aversion, or the mind that is always moving and changing, like a jumping flea or popping corn. To find the essence, we have to recognize the true nature of our body, speech, and mind, beyond our dreamlike experience of reality. The potential to do so exists only in a precious human birth with its unique combination of physical and mental capacities, opportunities, and propensity toward faith in the spiritual path.

If we use this life well, practicing with pure motivation and diligence, we might succeed in going beyond the cycles of suffering in a single lifetime so that we can benefit others without limitation. Otherwise, we may waste the great potential of our human body or, worse, create suffering for ourselves and others.

We can't assume that, having been human once, we'll be guaranteed a human existence again and again. A human body is very difficult to obtain. It requires the accumulation of a vast amount of merit through scrupulously pure discipline in past lifetimes. Discipline of this kind involves three things: not acting negatively or harmfully; cultivating virtuous thoughts and actions;

and in observing these first two disciplines, being motivated by the altruistic desire to benefit others. It is only because we have amassed sufficient merit, coupled with the aspiration to be reborn as a human being, that we find ourselves in the human realm.

Precious human birth provides a freedom and a leisure to practice not found in other realms of experience, either the three lower realms—the hell, hungry ghost, and animal realms—with their immense suffering, or the nonhuman higher realms—the jealous god (or demigod) and worldly god realms—with their false contentment.

"Precious human birth" does not refer to nominal human existence, in which one is born, lives, and dies, and then one's consciousness goes on to some other experience. A human rebirth is precious only when endowed with eight types of leisure and ten qualities and conditions.

The three lower realms afford no opportunity to hear or understand the teachings of dharma. Beings in these realms lack leisure or other supportive circumstances that aid or encourage practice; they experience too much suffering.

On the other hand, beings in the god realms have no incentive to practice. They are so infatuated with and intoxicated by sensual pleasures and bliss that the thought of escaping from this or any other state of cyclic existence never occurs to them.

In these five realms, there is neither the incentive nor opportunity to seek liberation from the cycles of samsaric suffering. In the human realm, however, we taste both sweet and sour. We know enough about suffering to want change, yet our suffering isn't so acute that we can't do anything about it.

Nonetheless, there are four types of human existence that lack sufficient leisure for practice. First, one might be born in a culture dominated by wrong view—the idea that killing or harming others is virtuous or spiritual, for example. Second, one might be adamantly skeptical about spirituality and religion. Neither intellectual sophistication nor scholarly learning necessarily leads to spiritual faith. Clever but cynical people find it difficult to put their trust in anything and thus don't have the openness and receptivity necessary for spiritual practice. Third, one might be born in a dark eon—an era in which no buddha manifests in the human realm to offer Buddhist or other beneficial spiritual teachings. Finally, one might be afflicted with a physical or mental handicap that makes it impossible to listen to or understand the teachings.

We need to realize that, not having been born in any of these situations, we enjoy a tremendous advantage. Our precious human birth provides us with freedom to practice. It also endows us with ten special qualities and conditions, five of which derive from who we are and five from outer circumstances.

The first five qualities include our human body itself, which can be a vehicle for attaining enlightenment; birth in an area where the teachings are available rather than in a "border country," where the influence of the dharma or other pure spiritual teachings has not spread; faculties that are intact and sufficient intelligence to enable us to understand the teachings; the blessings of a karmic predisposition to develop spiritually rather than waste this opportunity or use our life to harm others; and a receptivity to the Buddhist path or other spiritual traditions that offer short- and long-term benefit for ourselves and others.

The first of the five conditions deriving from outer circumstances is that a buddha has indeed appeared. Were we born into a universe where no buddha had ever manifested, the question of liberation wouldn't even come up, because we would have no historical example. By attaining enlightenment in our realm, the Buddha Shakyamuni demonstrated that it can be done.

The second condition is that, having appeared, the Buddha taught the dharma. Even though we might have the historical example of the Buddha, without his teachings there would be no path to follow.

The tradition of teachings that has been preserved and passed on throughout history is the third condition. Again, a buddha may appear and teach during a given generation, and beings may benefit, but the teachings might be lost or gradually die out. In our case, the Buddhist teachings have endured to this day.

The fourth condition arises from the presence of practitioners who have realized and provide a living example and transmission of the teachings.

Finally, due to the kindness and compassion of the lama, his willingness to teach and become involved with others rather than practice in solitude, we can learn, practice, and accomplish the teachings.

If we weren't endowed with all of these eighteen leisures and conditions, we couldn't even talk about the first of the four thoughts. We could never fulfill life's true purpose, never attain the goal of dispelling suffering and bringing about happiness for ourselves and others in both a temporary and an ultimate sense.

By continually contemplating the value of our precious human existence, we come to see that this birth is better than a wish-fulfilling gem. There are many stories of those who go to immense trouble, traveling long distances, enduring all kinds of hardships and life-threatening situations, to acquire such a gem; and yet at the end of their search what have they accomplished?

The gem's magic may make them wealthy for a while, find them an enchanting mate, or manifest a spacious home. But these last for only a certain amount of time. The gem can't produce enlightenment. With the skillful use of our human existence, we can not only realize short-term benefits, but also achieve liberation from samsara and help others to do so as well.

The fact that human existence is so rare becomes very clear when we compare the number of beings in the human realm with the number of those in the other five realms. Traditionally, it is said that hell beings are as countless as the dust particles in the entire universe. Hungry ghosts, slightly fewer in number, are said to be as numerous as the grains of sand in the river Ganges. As to animal life, there is no corner of land or drop of the ocean that isn't teeming with it—just as a container for making alcohol brims with grain. The number of beings in the demigod realm can be compared to the number of snowflakes in a blizzard, the number of beings in the human and worldly god realms to the number of dust particles on the surface of a thumbnail. Those endowed with a precious human birth, with the exalted aspiration to free all beings from suffering, are as rare as stars in the noonday sky.

The Buddha illustrated the rarity of precious human birth by comparing the three-thousand-fold universe to a huge ocean with a wooden yoke floating somewhere on top of it. The yoke is continually buffeted by wind, waves, and currents. At the bottom of the ocean lives a blind turtle that once every hundred years comes to the surface for a gulp of air, then goes back down to the bottom. The laws of chance dictate that, sooner or later, the wind will blow the yoke over the turtle in the same moment that he surfaces, and his head will poke through it. That this will happen is just barely conceivable. According to the Buddha, it is even less likely that someone will find a precious human birth.

Contemplating our great fortune again and again inspires us to practice with greater diligence and enthusiasm. If we knew that gold lay buried somewhere beneath us, we would dig for it with tremendous inspiration and continue until we found it. If we were told to dig without knowing the gold was there, why would we bother? Once we appreciate that our precious human birth is extremely rare, that it provides a unique opportunity for liberation, we begin to understand that we should not waste it but rather fulfill its deeper purpose—to reveal the essence of our existence, the true nature of mind.

9

Impermanence

TO UNDERSTAND THE ROOT of suffering, we have to acknowledge that nothing in life is permanent. We perceive phenomena, including our physical body and everything we experience with our senses, to be solid and lasting, habitually clinging to things and making plans as if they might last forever. Yet nothing stays the same; everything changes easily, constantly.

Meditating continually on this truth is one of the best methods for developing pure spiritual practice. We begin by looking at the inanimate universe. At some point eons ago, there was nothing here. In Buddhist cosmology, the element of wind appeared first, giving rise to the elements of fire, then water and earth, as the physical universe came into being, with Mount Meru in the center surrounded by the four continents. Then life forms began to arise, first from cellular division, then from various kinds of asexual, then sexual reproduction, including egg and womb birth.

This vast period of creation culminated in the present "era of duration," during which there will be eighteen cycles of increasing and decreasing well-being and happiness. As the universe nears its end and the physical environment is no longer conducive to life, more and more beings will be reborn in other universes.

Finally, physical matter will disintegrate until, once again, none of it remains.

As we ponder these things, our perception of the universe will start to change. We will realize that, no matter how true and reliable it may seem, it is not eternal. On a smaller scale, we will see that mountain ranges have come and gone, and where huge oceans once surged, only dry land remains. Once-flourishing towns have given way to empty wasteland, and on former wasteland, huge cities have grown up. We will become conscious of unending change in our environment, from prehistoric time through recorded history.

Change is continuous. Day by day one season slips into the next. Day turns into night and night into day. Buildings don't suddenly deteriorate; rather, they do so second by second, from the moment they are constructed.

Our environment, physical body, speech, and thoughts change as swiftly as a needle piercing a rose petal. If we pierce a pile of cupped rose petals with a needle, it may seem to be a single movement, but it actually consists of many discrete steps. We penetrate each petal separately, going through its outside edge, through the middle, out the other side, through the space between that petal and the next, through one side of the next, and so on. The time it takes the needle to pass through each of those successive stages is sometimes used as a way of describing the rate of change of all phenomena in our world.

Think of the beings inhabiting this universe. How many people born a hundred years ago are still alive? How many of us now on this earth will be here a hundred years from today? Historic figures—no matter how rich they were, how famous, how successful, how much territory they controlled—are now only legends. A story is often told in the Buddhist teachings of a king so powerful he controlled not only the known world but the realm of Indra, king of the gods. Yet only his legend remains.

Extraordinary masters of the past—the eight great dharma kings, the twenty-five principal disciples of the great teacher Padmasambhava, even the Buddha Shakyamuni, a manifestation of supreme compassion in human form—are no longer here. This doesn't mean that their blessings died with their physical bodies, for the positive qualities of enlightened mind pervade the three times of past, present, and future. But from our individual perspective, those beings have disappeared, just as when the world turns it appears to us that the sun has set.

We see the play of impermanence in our relationships as well. How many of our family members, friends, or people in our hometown have died? How many have moved away, gone from our lives forever?

As little children, we couldn't bear to be away from our parents. Sometimes, when our mother left the room for two or three minutes, we panicked. Now we may not write to our parents more than once a year. Perhaps they live on the other side of the world. We might not even know whether they are alive. How things have changed!

At one time we felt happy just being near a person we loved. Just to hold his hand made us feel wonderful. Now maybe we can't stand him or don't want to know anything about him. Whatever comes together must fall apart, what was once gathered must separate, whoever was born must die. Continuous and relentless change defines our world.

"So," you might think, "the universe incessantly changes, and likewise relationships, yet 'I' am always the same." But what is "I"? Is it the body? After conception, the human body begins as a single cell, which divides into a cell mass that, in turn, differentiates into various organ systems. After coming into the world as an infant, we undergo the continual process of growing and developing into an adult. This takes place week by week, month by month, and year by year until eventually we realize that things are getting worse rather than better. We are no longer growing up; we are aging. Inevitably, we lose certain capacities: our eyesight fails, our hearing fades, our thinking becomes muddled. This is impermanence taking its toll.

If we live a normal life span, we'll become more and more feeble, until one day we won't be able to get out of bed. Perhaps we won't be able to feed or clothe ourselves or recognize those around us. At a certain point we'll die, our body an empty shell, our mind wandering in the bardo, the intermediate state between death and rebirth. This body, so important to us for so long, will be cremated or buried. It might even be devoured by wild animals or birds. At a certain point we'll be nothing more than a memory.

"Well," you might think, "the body is impermanent, but the 'real me,' my mind, is not." However, if you look at your mind, you will see that it isn't the same as it was when you were an infant. Then, all you wanted was your mother's milk and a warm place to sleep. A little later a few toys made you happy. Later it was a girlfriend or boyfriend, and still later a certain job or marriage or home. Your needs, desires, and values have changed, not all at once but by degree. Even throughout each day, the mind experiences happiness and sadness, virtuous and nonvirtuous thoughts, many times over. If we try to grasp one particular moment, even as we think to grasp it, it disappears.

Like our body and mind, our speech is constantly changing: every word we utter is lost, another rushing to replace it. There is nothing we can point to as unchanging, stable, or permanent.

We need to instill in ourselves an ongoing, moment-by-moment awareness of impermanence, for life is a race against death and the time of death remains unknown. Contemplating the approach of death changes our priorities and helps us to let go of our obsession with ordinary involvements. If we remain aware that each moment might be our last, we will intensify our practice, not wanting to waste or misuse our precious human opportunity. As our contemplation of this truth deepens, we will have some comprehension of how the world works, how appearances arise and change. We will move from a mere intellectual understanding of impermanence to a more experiential realization that everything we have based our belief of reality upon is just the shimmering radiance of change. We will begin to see that everything is illusory, like a dream or mirage; though phenomena appear, in truth nothing substantial is really there. This will help us to grasp the most profound Buddhist teachings.

What then, we might ask, will be of benefit to us when we die? It doesn't matter how pleasant or congenial people think we are; after we're dead they won't want our body around. Nor will they be able to go with us, no matter who they are or how happy they have made us. We all die alone, whether we are famous or as wealthy as the god of wealth himself. At the time of our death, all the possessions we have accumulated, all the power, status, and fame we have achieved, all the friends we have gathered—none of it will be of any help to us. Our consciousness will be plucked from our body as cleanly as a hair from butter. Only our practice of the dharma will benefit us; only our positive and negative karma will follow us at death. Nothing else.

QUESTION: If we contemplate impermanence like this, won't we become apathetic to the needs of others?

RESPONSE: Our intention on the spiritual path is to relieve the suffering of others as much as and in every way we can, until we are ultimately able to relieve all beings of suffering. At the same time, we maintain an awareness of impermanence in everything we do, remembering that, like a dream, everyday life occurs but isn't inherently true. In this context, we do everything possible to benefit others and to reduce the mind's poisons so that we won't harm ourselves or others. If we practice virtue and reduce non-virtue, this dream we call life will improve. Remembering the dreamlike and impermanent nature of our experience, we will eventually wake up and help others to do so as well.

As our realization of impermanence and the illusory nature of reality increases, so does our compassion. We see that, trapped by their belief in the dream and having no understanding of impermanence, beings suffer tremendous anguish. Because they believe in the solidity of their experience, they react to their arising karma with attachment and aversion, making more negative karma and perpetuating the cycles of suffering.

QUESTION: What is the difference between contemplating impermanence and looking at your watch, wondering how soon whatever you're doing will be finished?

RESPONSE: It comes down to motivation. If your motivation is selfless, you won't notice the clock much. If it isn't, then things will seem to take longer than you'd expect. I wouldn't discourage you from clock watching, but watch samsara's clock: ask yourself how soon samsara will be finished. Then the question becomes, "How can I cut attachment? How can I cut aversion? How can I cut confusion?" By eliminating the mind's obscurations, we can eventually bring samsara to an end.

QUESTION: I have a great fear that belief in the illusory nature of everything will create more, not less, suffering because we'll let go of everything that matters. Sometimes when things are difficult, all we have left is hope. If we let go of hope, we have nothing.

RESPONSE: Just because someone fears that a certain medicine is toxic and will cause more illness doesn't mean that this is true or that the medicine won't help. Many of us trapped in samsara tend to fear the medicine we need more than our predicament. We fear facing the truth of our experience because we want to believe that everything is stable, that it will last. But nothing stays the same—no one has ever escaped sickness, old age, or death, no matter how vehement his denial.

We suffer not because our experience is illusory, but because we deny that it is. If we recognize the illusory nature of things and face up to the inevitability of our death, we will set priorities and make choices that will produce happiness, rather than suffering, for ourselves and others.

Misplaced hope will only cause suffering. If we convince ourselves that the donkey in the yard is a lion and place our hope for protection on it, we'll be in trouble when a wolf attacks. On the spiritual path, we place our hope on something reliable—

spiritual methods that can take us beyond suffering. We hope that they will produce change, that they will help us with our difficulties and create benefit, until enlightenment. We use hope to transform hope.

QUESTION: I agree with some of what you're saying, but my life is really busy. I don't see how contemplating impermanence would help me change my priorities so that I have more time to practice. I have a family that depends on me, a job, and so forth.

RESPONSE: If, after following the spiritual path for many years, you don't have a strong practice, then you haven't contemplated impermanence enough. Think carefully about what really matters now; ask yourself what you will leave behind and what you will take with you when you die. Even if you were to find a hidden treasure, you couldn't take it along. Your practice, though, is like special currency that will go with you across the border of death, lifetime after lifetime.

If you say that you have no time for meditation, you don't truly understand impermanence. You may work eight hours a day, but you still have sixteen hours left. Claiming that you don't have time, that you have responsibility for children and a job, is no excuse. The great dharma king Indrabhuti ruled over an entire kingdom yet managed to attain enlightenment in a single lifetime. Very few of us have as many responsibilities as he did. If we are diligent, we can always find enough time. If not, we'll always find a reason not to practice. It is only after we die that we won't have time. Until then, even if we're sick or busy, we have time.

QUESTION: I still find that the weight of my many years of not thinking this way is stronger than my belief in the teaching on impermanence. How can I change this habit?

RESPONSE: Let's start with a simple exercise. Examine the importance you place on the food you eat, your clothes, your house, your friends, your conversations, the books you read. You'll probably find that you hold them to be so indispensable that you work night and day to maintain them.

Now examine these things closely. Look at each in turn and ask yourself whether it is permanent. Ask yourself whether it is something you can ultimately depend on. At the hour of your death and beyond, will it be reliable? And is it worth all the effort and concern that you devote to it now? Thinking about impermanence and death helps to cut through worldly values and changes your priorities.

By contemplating and applying these teachings in each moment of your life, you will change your habits. You won't do so simply by reading books. You must probe, question, and examine. You may already have been exposed to all kinds of ideas and understand many things intellectually, but without the contemplation that deepens your practice and allows you to reach some very fundamental conclusions, you won't be able to take the next step.

To discover what's really important to you, spend a few minutes now reflecting on what I've said and examining how it relates to your own experience. Only through contemplation will you find out whether spiritual practice has heart and meaning for you.

10

Karma

ALTHOUGH SOME PEOPLE think the principle of karma exists only in Buddhist doctrine, it can actually be found in almost all spiritual traditions. It is usually stated simply: "If you are good, you'll go to heaven, you'll be happy. If you are bad, you'll go to hell, you'll suffer." In these traditions, the principle of inevitable consequence we call karma is like a train with only two destinations, heaven and hell. The Buddhist view is that the train makes many stops in between. The greater one's goodness, the greater one's experience of happiness. The greater one's negativity, the greater one's suffering and pain. Our present everyday reality is the karmic outcome of our thoughts, words, and deeds in this and former lifetimes.

Some people have difficulty with Buddhism's more extensive view of karma because they don't believe in reincarnation. Since they can't verify that they or anyone else will have a future existence or that they've had any previous ones, they can't accept the idea of rebirth. But the fact that we can't remember past lives or glimpse future ones is not a sufficient reason for not believing in them. There are many things we have confidence in though we can't see or empirically verify them. Like tomorrow! We can't prove that tomorrow is going to happen, but we're willing to bet that it will. People can't prove that at a certain age they're going to retire, live off whatever they've set aside, relax and have a good time, yet many are saving for that. In the same way, the inability to remember or foresee other lifetimes doesn't mean they didn't or won't exist.

Karma is like a seed that, under the proper conditions, will yield a plant. If you sow a barley seed, you can be certain you'll get a barley shoot. The seed won't produce rice.

The mind is like a fertile field—all sorts of things can grow there. When we plant a seed—an action, a statement, or a thought—it will eventually produce fruit, which will ripen, fall to the ground, and generate more of the same. Every moment, we plant potent seeds of causality with our body, speech, and mind. When the right conditions come together and our karma ripens, we will have to deal with the consequences of what we have planted.

Although we are responsible for what we sow, we forget what we've planted and either give credit to or blame people or things outside of us when they ripen. We're like a bird perched on a rock who can see its shadow but, when it flies away, forgets that the shadow exists. Each time it lands, the bird thinks it has found a completely different shadow. In the moment, we have a thought, we speak or act. But we lose sight of the fact that each thought, word, and action will produce a result. When the fruit finally ripens, we think, "Why did this happen to me? I've done nothing to deserve this."

Once we have committed a negative action, unless it is purified, we will experience its consequences. We can't deny our responsibility or try to make the karma disappear by justifying what we've done. It doesn't work that way. Whoever commits an act will infallibly experience its results, whether positive or negative.

Every movement of our thoughts, words, and deeds is like a thread in the fabric of our unfolding reality. Latent in our present experience are oceans of karma from countless past lifetimes, which under the proper conditions will come to fruition.

In order to find liberation from samsara, we must work at the causal level rather than the level of results—the pleasure and pain that are the consequences of our behavior. To do so, we need to purify our earlier mistakes and the mental poisons that perpetuate karma and change the mind that plants the seeds of suffering. This process is called "closing the door of nonvirtue," averting karmic consequences by taking preventive measures, no longer committing actions tainted by the faults of the mind.

We speak of positive, negative, and neutral karma. Acts that generate positive karma lead to personal happiness and happiness for others. Negative karma brings about suffering for ourselves and others. When our intention is to benefit others, our thoughts, words, and actions are virtuous and create positive karma. When we are motivated by the mind's poisons, our thoughts, words, and actions are nonvirtuous and create negative karma. Innocuous actions, those motivated neither by the desire to harm nor by the intention to help, create neutral karma. Because such karma doesn't have a positive effect, it is often considered nonvirtuous, which is why karma is sometimes referred to only as positive or negative.

Altruistic motivation can produce both exhaustible and inexhaustible virtue or benefit. We create exhaustible virtue when our motivation is to benefit others but our frame of reference is limited. If we feed a hungry person or nurse someone sick, and our goal doesn't include helping that person and all beings awaken from the cycles of suffering, the happiness we experience as a result of our meritorious action will be temporary. It will end when the good karma we have created is exhausted. It won't lead to liberation from samsara.

When we undertake an action with the intention that a particular person, as well as all other beings, not only find temporary happiness but awaken from cyclic existence, we produce inexhaustible virtue or benefit. This results not only in happiness in the higher realms of experience, but ultimately in enlightenment.

We need to become absolutely certain of the infallibility of the karmic process constantly at work in our lives. Our endless suffering, our experiences of higher and lower states of rebirth, are rooted in the inexorable unfolding of good and bad karma.

There was once a hermit who lived and meditated in a forest. He had only one set of clothes, which over time began to fade. One day he decided to dye them, so he heated a pot of water, and placed the clothes and dye into it.

Meanwhile, a farmer was searching the area for a lost calf. He saw the smoke from the hermit's fire and immediately assumed that somebody had stolen and slaughtered his calf and was cooking it. He came upon the pot and, finding no one around, looked inside. There he saw the boiling head and limbs of the calf. He ran to the king, crying, "This man claiming to be a great sage is nothing but a common thief. He stole my calf and is busy cooking it for his dinner right now." The king was outraged: this so-called sage who had been living in his domain, gathering students, teaching, and gaining fame and respect, had turned out to be a thief. He sent his soldiers to arrest the hermit and throw him into prison.

Actually, the calf had only wandered off, and after seven days found its way back to the farmer, alive and well. Very contrite, the farmer went straight to the king and confessed, "This is terrible! I've slandered this great saint. Please let him out of prison immediately." The king agreed to do so but, being very busy, forgot all about it.

Seven months later, the sage was still in jail. Finally, one of his students, who possessed great meditative powers, flew through the air to the king and said, "My teacher has done nothing wrong. Please let him go!" The king instantly remembered and went to the dungeon himself to release the hermit. He was overcome with remorse, not only for having arrested him without due process, but for having forgotten to let him out.

The hermit told the king, "You've nothing to be sorry for. This was my karma. In a previous lifetime I stole and killed a calf. As I was running away from the owner, I came across a holy person meditating in the forest. I thought I would place the blame on him by dumping the carcass outside his hut and running away. He was wrongly accused and thrown in prison for seven days. The consequences of that action were so negative that my mindstream underwent rebirth after rebirth in lower realms of existence. Now, having attained this human life, I have been able to continue my spiritual development. But some residual karma had to be purified. From my point of view, things have turned out very well."

It is crucial that we discern what is virtuous and nonvirtuous. Otherwise, even as practitioners trying to be of benefit, we may actually create more harm than good. The subtle flaw of pride might arise: "I'm a very spiritual person," or "My tradition is the best one," or "Those poor folks who don't have a spiritual path!" Whenever we make such judgments, we only produce negative karma. If we fail to use our body, speech, and mind in a careful, disciplined way, our flaws can increase. Our minds are rife with the five poisons. With these paints in our palette, what kind of picture will we create?

We produce physical nonvirtue through killing, stealing, or sexual misconduct. A fully nonvirtuous action has four parts. For example, killing includes identifying the object to be killed; establishing the motivation to kill; committing the act of killing; and bringing about the result, the victim's death. If we have the intention to kill someone but don't carry through with it, we still generate half the nonvirtue by identifying the object and establishing the motivation to kill. Or if in walking down the sidewalk we accidentally step on an ant and kill it, we also create half the nonvirtue of killing.

Stealing means taking something that hasn't been given to us. It includes taking something without the owner knowing it, overpowering a person in order to appropriate something, or using a position of power or authority to seize something from another in order to benefit oneself.

Sexual misconduct involves sexual activity with someone underage, with someone who is sick, or when such activity will cause mental or emotional distress or the breaking of one's own or another's vows or commitment to a sexual partner.

The four nonvirtues of speech are: lying, the worst lie being that of falsely claiming that one has spiritual realization; slander, which involves using speech to separate close friends, the worst case being that of slandering members of one's spiritual group; harsh speech that hurts others; and gossip or useless speech, which wastes one's own and others' time.

The first of the three nonvirtues of the mind is covetousness. The second nonvirtue consists of harmful thoughts: wanting to harm another, wishing that another might be harmed, or rejoicing in harm done to another. The third is wrong view, thinking in very contrary ways, as opposed to doubting and questioning, which are healthy components of spiritual contemplation. Believing that it is good to be bad, or bad to be good, is an example of wrong view. So is not accepting the illusory nature of experience because we can't prove it, thus denying the basic truth that will ultimately produce liberation from suffering. Although we may not be able to prove that our experience is illusory, neither can we prove that it isn't.

The ten virtues follow clearly from the ten nonvirtues. Saving and protecting life, for example, creates tremendous virtue. All beings seek happiness, strive to avoid suffering, and value their lives as much as we do. To save the life of even an insect or an animal is extremely virtuous and, when the merit is dedicated, creates great benefit not only for that animal but for all beings. Merit dedicated to the long life of others, for example, can be of immense benefit to those who are sick.

Generosity, no matter how seemingly insignificant—even giving a bit of food or water to a hungry bird—produces great virtue. Maintaining discipline in sexual relationships, telling the truth, using gentle speech to create harmony and benefit for oneself and others, as well as rejoicing in the happiness of others, generating helpful and kind thoughts, and maintaining correct view—these are all virtues.

The karmic fruit of an act is similar whether you commit the act yourself, ask someone else to, or rejoice when others do. If you recite one hundred mantras alone, you create the virtue of reciting that number of mantras. But if a group of ten people recite one hundred mantras, each member of the group creates the virtue of reciting a thousand mantras. Similarly, if a person in an angry mob kills someone, everyone in the mob generates the same nonvirtue.

Although it may appear that our situation is hopeless, through confession and purification, we can avert the negative karma we have accumulated from beginningless time. It is said that the only virtue of nonvirtue is that it can be purified.

When I was a little boy, a woman came to visit my mother. She wore a necklace with a flat, luminous object dangling from it. Fascinated, I asked her what it was.

"A fish bone," she replied.

I wanted it! I had to have one like it! So I ran to the river and caught a small fish, thinking there must be a beautiful bone inside it. I put the fish down and took out my knife. I couldn't stand to look as I tried to cut the fish, so I turned my face away. But my knife was dull and I couldn't make the fish die. It just flopped around on the ground and finally died. When it stopped moving, I cut it open and looked inside. There was no bone like the one the woman wore around her neck.

Chagrined, I returned home and told the lady, "I looked inside a fish, but I couldn't find a bone like this."

"No, no, no," she said. "You can only find such a bone in fishes that live in the big ocean."

It was then that I realized that perhaps I had done something wrong. I had killed a fish and it wasn't even the right kind.

Later, when I was twenty-two years old and in my second three-year meditation retreat, I had a dream in which I gazed out over a huge expanse of water. The sky and the water met. I'd never seen anything like that in landlocked Tibet, not even in a picture. I asked, "What is this?" Someone in the dream said, "This is where you will be reborn." Then I remembered the fish and realized that this was the karma I had created by killing it. I prayed, "If I am going to be reborn a fish, let me be a little fish so that I won't make more bad karma by eating other fish."

When I awoke very early the next morning, a fish appeared in the dark in front of me. Everywhere I turned, the fish was there. I couldn't get away from it. I began to recite the mantra *Om Mani Padme Hung* in the breaks between my retreat practice sessions, dedicating the virtue of my practice to the fish I'd killed. After I had finished a million recitations, the fish finally disappeared. I think now I may have purified my fish karma.

We don't need to know exactly what karma we are purifying to apply a particular method; purification techniques address all manner of negative karma. The development of compassion and loving kindness, selflessness, meditation on and prayer to enlightened beings, the recitation of mantra—all of these help to diminish our present suffering, to make us more careful in our practice of harmlessness, and to purify the causes of future suffering.

However, if while doing purification practice we think, "I have so much bad karma to purify" or "I really want to attain buddhahood," our motivation isn't pure. Such self-interested practice is less effective than arousing pure compassion outside of formal practice sessions. The most effective approach of all is formal practice based on compassion and the intention to liberate every being from samsara. Whenever we bring forth good heart, helpfulness, love, and compassion, such qualities, like a solvent, naturally purify and dissolve karma.

The great Indian Buddhist practitioner Asanga went into retreat in a cave and meditated night and day on Maitreya Buddha. After six years, he hadn't had a single auspicious dream or vision—no sign of accomplishment. So Asanga decided that his meditation was futile. He left his cave and, as he walked down the road, passed a man rubbing a silk scarf on an iron pillar. Asanga asked the man, "Sir, what are you doing?"

"I'm making a needle," the man replied.

Asanga thought, "Oh, such perseverance! He's rubbing an iron pillar with a silk scarf to make a needle, and I don't even have enough patience to stay in retreat." He walked back to his cave and started meditating again, night and day, on the Buddha Maitreya.

After three more years of meditation, he still had received no sign of accomplishment—no dream, no vision, nothing. Again, very discouraged, he left his retreat. As he walked down the road, he saw a man dipping a feather into a bucket of water and brushing the rock face of a huge cliff. Asanga asked the man what he was doing.

"This cliff is casting a shadow on my house," he replied, "so I am removing it."

Asanga thought, "Here is someone who, for just a little sunshine on his roof, would stand endlessly brushing a rock face away. And I don't even have enough diligence to meditate until I get a sign." So he went back to his cave and sat down to meditate.

After a total of twelve years in retreat, he still had received no sign. Again, discouraged and disappointed, he left. Walking down the road this time, he encountered a very sick dog. The lower half of her body was rotten with gangrene and filled with maggots. Missing her two hind legs, she could only drag herself along the road, yet she turned and snapped at everyone around her. Asanga's heart moved. "This poor dog," he thought. "What can I do to help her? I have to clean the wound, but then I might kill the maggots. I cannot take the life of one to preserve the life of another; every life has value."

Finally he decided that by carefully licking the maggots away from the wound he could save both the insects and the dog. It was a revolting idea, but he closed his eyes and leaned over. When he opened his mouth, his tongue touched not the animal but the ground. He opened his eyes. The dog was gone and there stood the Buddha Maitreya.

"I've been praying to you for years and years," Asanga exclaimed, "and this is the first time you've appeared!"

The Buddha replied very kindly, "Since the very first day of your retreat, I have been with you. But because of the delusion caused by your nonvirtue and the poisons of your mind, you couldn't see me. I was the man rubbing the pillar, and I was the man brushing the cliff. Not until I appeared as this pathetic dog did you have enough compassion and selflessness to purify the karma that kept you from seeing me."

Karma can also be purified through sincere confession and regret, utilizing the *four powers*. The first of these is the power of witness or support. We invoke the embodiment of perfection in whom we have faith, a particular aspect of enlightened being such as Tara, the embodiment of wisdom, or Vajrasattva, the deity of purification, as the witness of our practice.

The second power is that of regret for all of our negative actions in this and every previous lifetime—not only for specific incidents that we remember, but for the whole backlog of harmful acts we've committed since beginningless time. We recognize these actions as harmful and accept responsibility for them. Our regret must be sincere, as if we suddenly realized we had mistakenly swallowed some deadly poison. We feel anguish over our ignorance of the moral consequences of our actions and over having acted carelessly for countless lifetimes in ways that will only result in suffering.

The third power is the firm decision not to commit any negative actions in the future. We can't spend the day indulging in negative thoughts and actions and then, at night, expect to purify them with a little meditation practice. Instead, we must make a sincere commitment never to repeat them. A famous Tibetan Buddhist prayer affirms that without regret and firm resolve, confession is not effective.

The fourth power is that of the antidote: the purification and blessing. We visualize nectar or rays of light flowing from the object of our faith through our body and purifying us, washing away all negativity, sickness, and obscuration.

In Buddhist India some centuries ago, a nun named Palmo was afflicted with leprosy. With no effective treatment known, her body began to rot and waste away. She repeatedly performed a very strong purification practice, the two-day fasting ritual of the bodhisattva of compassion, Avalokiteshvara. After a long period of time, she had a vision of Avalokiteshvara and was completely cured. She had purified the karma that had resulted in her horrible disease.

Until recently in Tibet, there wasn't an effective treatment for leprosy. People with this affliction were isolated from everyone else, and food brought to them was left at a distance. When a leper died, nobody dared to bury or even touch the body. Instead, the leper's house was collapsed onto the corpse.

A Tibetan lama with leprosy performed the same two-day fasting ritual of Avalokiteshvara a thousand times in succession and was cured.

Through diligent practice, eons of karma can be purified in a single lifetime; otherwise the ripening and purification of karma are drawn out lifetime after lifetime.

QUESTION: If someone who has lived a virtuous life has an accident and experiences a great deal of hardship, it is difficult to see how that misfortune is a result of a negative action the person committed five thousand lifetimes ago. It doesn't seem fair.

RESPONSE: If we plant rice, wheat, and barley indiscriminately in a field, we can't really complain about the confusion of grains growing there at harvest time. If we don't want them, we shouldn't have planted them in the first place. Whenever a seed is planted, the result is inevitable. So instead of becoming upset at harvest time, we need to learn to be more careful during planting season.

In a previous lifetime we ourselves committed the negative actions that have led to our present suffering. It won't be of any use to cry out now, claiming that what is happening to us isn't fair. The point is to engage in actions that will produce favorable results, not to dwell on the inevitable results of former negative actions.

Our past actions account not only for our suffering but for our happiness as well. The problem is that we want only our positive karma to unfold. But if we want only good fruit to ripen, we should plant only good seeds.

QUESTION: Does karma explain the killing of innocent children in war?

RESPONSE: Generally, everything is the result of some karmic predisposition or tendency. But not all karmic tendencies are of equal force—some are more powerful than others. Children who are killed in war did nothing in their present lifetime to justify their death. But to have been born when and where they were, and killed under those circumstances, they must in a previous lifetime have created the karma to die in that way. This does not mean they deserve to die, but it explains why there are "innocent victims."

QUESTION: Some people respond passively to the law of karma. When something negative happens to them, they simply say it is their fate. How do we accept the truth of karma and at the same time work actively with our problems?

RESPONSE: Because we create our own karma, we have the power to purify it. If we find that we don't like a story we wrote long ago, we can rewrite it. We do this in a spiritual sense by confessing and purifying previous harmful actions and vowing never to commit them again, invoking the four powers while praying or reciting mantra. We also undertake virtuous actions that will create a new story line for the future.

QUESTION: There are so many beings and so much karma, how is it all arranged? How is it all kept track of? How does it work?

RESPONSE: It isn't a process that needs keeping track of. Actions work themselves out in their own way without anyone controlling the outcome. It is not as though someone has to keep a record of everything so that everyone goes to the right realm, and so forth. A being's actions determine that being's eventual experience.

QUESTION: Does karma always ripen in the same way?

RESPONSE: Karma is more complex than that. There is what we call the *complete maturation* of a karmic tendency. Virtuous actions, those that contribute to the happiness of others, benefit the person who performs them, either in this or in some future lifetime. Such actions contribute to rebirth in higher states of existence. Conversely, harmful acts that bring about pain and suffering result in rebirth in lower realms.

There are also the karmic consequences known as *behavior in harmony with the initial action*. Consider a predatory animal, a hunter, or a soldier—a being who kills others. The complete maturation of this tendency to kill is rebirth in a hell realm. Once the karma has been exhausted, that being, owing to other virtuous karma, may attain a human rebirth and yet still have a habit of killing. Taking many lives results in a predisposition or compulsion to kill. As this pattern is reinforced, it leads to more negative karma and negative habits, like a snowball that grows larger as it rolls down a hill.

On the other hand, some young children demonstrate love and caring toward small animals or insects. Such qualities have been developed in previous lifetimes through training in love and compassion and will continue to grow if the child receives further training.

Then there is *experience that accords directly with the initial action*. Someone may kill many beings and as a result be born in a hell realm. Much later, he may attain a human rebirth, but his life will be short or even terminated violently.

A single act has a multitude of potential consequences. It's not that we commit one act, then go on to another realm and pay the consequences, and then come back again to the human realm.

The point is that whether we committed a harmful action in a previous lifetime or in this one, we unavoidably created negative karma. We can't escape that fact, even though perhaps there are aspects of it we are not aware of right now.

QUESTION: Is there such a thing as group karma?

RESPONSE: The mind is the source of all karma, including group karma. Those with similar karma share a collective reality, including their physical and social environment. Humans have one kind of collective reality, animals another. Yet within their common experience, individuals encounter different phenomena—some pleasurable, some painful. Because of similar karma, a number of people may live in a war zone, but not all of them will suffer to the same degree, not all will die. It is mainly individuals' personal karma that determines their circumstances.

QUESTION: What can I do about cockroaches in my home?

RESPONSE: There is no easy answer. Tibetans say that if you drop a hot clay pot it will break, but if you hold it your hands will burn.

If you can, it's best to remove insects from your home without hurting them. I haven't had any personal experience with cockroaches, but I have with ants. One of my students developed a method for removing them from our center. He created an ant pureland: a big bucket filled with rotten wood and a mixture of honey and water. He made a trail of the mixture from the building to the bucket. One by one, the ants were drawn to the bucket. When it was full, he took it to the forest and let them go. He repeated the process until all the ants were gone.

Do everything possible not to kill, because the karma of killing even one insect can cause you grave suffering in the future. Karma involves the principle of multiplication. Just as one apple seed grows into a tree with many apples, one act that causes suffering will produce hundreds of times more suffering for the harm doer in the future. If you kill another being, even inadvertently, use the four powers of confession to purify the karma and then dedicate the merit to those you have killed.

QUESTION: What about all the nonvirtue we unknowingly create every day by eating meat or wearing cotton clothing when insects have been killed to harvest that cotton?

RESPONSE: It's true that, in order for us to eat or drink, other beings are often harmed. Some vegetarians think that they bear no responsibility for the death of living beings. Yet in the planting and harvesting of grains, vegetables, and teas, many animals that live in the ground are killed when the earth is turned, and many others drown when the crops are watered. We in the Tibetan highlands used to feel great compassion for the people of the lowlands who consumed a lot of grains and vegetables, because of the many insects that died so they could eat. When we ate yak meat, a staple of our diet, only one being had to die to feed many people for many meals.

In the refugee camps in India where we lived after fleeing the Chinese occupation of Tibet, we worked in tea factories and saw many insects die as each leaf was harvested. It is difficult to live without hurting others, but we can begin by trying not to harm. In eating either meat or vegetables, at least we haven't engaged in three of the four aspects of nonvirtuous action: identifying the victims, establishing the motivation to kill them, and either ordering or enacting the killing. Our only nonvirtue is our rejoicing in their death through our consumption of the food, and in this we share the nonvirtue of the person who actually caused the death.

In addition to not intentionally causing harm, we can dedicate whatever merit we create to all those beings with whom we have either a positive or negative connection—in this case to those with whom we have a negative connection through eating, drinking, or wearing clothing of natural fibers—so that they will experience both temporary and ultimate benefit. Then our relationship with these beings may become their connection to the path of liberation. We can even sponsor practitioners in retreat to do special purification practices and dedicate the merit to the beings we've harmed.

Somebody once asked a great practitioner about his past life, saying, "You must have been a very high lama or practiced great virtue to have developed such realization in this life." The practitioner replied, "Not at all. In my last life I was a goat with no previous connection to the dharma. But a great yogi prayed strongly on my behalf before eating my body, and my practice in this life is a result of those prayers."

Purifying karma through spiritual practice doesn't require leaving our worldly lives behind. Rather, by integrating practice into our daily activities and resting in mind's true nature, we can purify all our accumulated karma in one lifetime.

11

The Ocean of Suffering

THE RESULTS OF ALL our actions form the tapestry of our lives—every thread, every detail. Each of us continues to weave different physical and environmental realities, binding ourselves inextricably to the cycles of suffering. Our experience depends on our karma, which produces differing degrees of delusion. If the mind's poisons are acute, we endure a very painful, hellish reality. If the poisons decrease, our reality becomes less harsh, more pleasant.

The Buddha spoke of suffering as one would speak of illness to the sick—to help them understand their ailment and potential treatments. If there were no remedy for suffering, there would be no point in discussing it. But because there is a remedy, it is important that we recognize suffering as fundamental so we can begin to address it.

There are three kinds of suffering. The first is the *suffering of change*. Nothing is reliable or consistent. No matter how much we hope for a firm foundation to stand on, whatever we rely upon always erodes, creating great pain. The second kind is *suffering atop suffering*. One bad thing happens after another, and there seems to be no fairness to it. Whenever we think that our situation can't get any worse, it does. We lose wealth, family members, vitality—there are countless ways in which we suffer. The third is *pervasive suffering*. Just as when you squeeze a sesame seed, you find that it's pervaded with oil, it may seem that our lives are happy, but under the pressure of our ripening karma, we suffer. As surely as we're born, we will become sick, age, and die.

Within samsara, there are countless beings whose suffering is far greater than ours. Ninety-five percent experience a brutal reality. The lives of only five percent—humans, demigods, and worldly gods—are relatively fortunate. Yet we humans often bemoan our existence, complaining bitterly about our terrible problems. We would not do so if we truly understood the tremendous degree of suffering pervading other realms. The very worst human experience is still a thousand times more bearable than that of the least-suffering beings in the lower realms. Their suffering is so extreme that we can scarcely imagine it; the length of time it lasts is unfathomable. For some beings, even death provides no escape until hundreds of thousands of years, sometimes eons, have passed.

Most beings in these realms have no opportunity to help themselves. Their suffering is so intense, they haven't a moment's leisure to meditate or to examine themselves or their lives from a different point of view. Other beings, in higher realms, are intoxicated with pleasure. False contentment prevents them from using their ample leisure to create conditions for future happiness. As their long lives inevitably come to an end and they see their future rebirths in lower realms, they experience terrible suffering.

The idea that we can experience a realm of suffering like hell makes many people skeptical or contemptuous. They don't believe in hell; they think the concept is just a scare tactic some religions use to control people. In a sense, it's true that there is no hell. If we put all the world's technology to use trying to reach the center of the earth, we'd never find hell. Yet many beings are suffering in the hell realms at this very moment.

Hell is the reflection of mind's delusion, of angry thoughts and intentions and the harmful words and actions they produce. If we don't control these, we will unavoidably experience hell. Practitioners have to be careful; some might think, "My meditation is so profound I don't have to worry about karma." But the repercussions of delusion are infallible, and it doesn't take a lot of delusion to find oneself reborn in hell.

Some people experience hell even while in a human body. Many of them fill our hospitals. There are people who are tormented by the belief that someone is trying to kill them or tear their flesh. There are some who experience being eaten alive or being trapped in a fire. We could be sitting in the same room with them and see nothing of what they endure. At the same time, we might be standing right beside a great meditator who is experiencing heaven, the pureland, without seeing it ourselves.

Heaven and hell, in fact, aren't really so far apart. This is not easy to understand, since the experience of heaven is very different from that of hell. But it makes sense if we consider the example of a simple substance like water. To humans, water is crucial for sustaining life; to fish, it is their very environment; to worldly gods, an ambrosia-like substance; to hungry ghosts, blood or pus; to hell beings, molten lava. It's not that the substance itself differs in each case, but rather that different beings' perceptions and experiences of it vary. Just as our vision changes when we put on prescription glasses, our experience of reality is affected by our perception, which is determined by the extent of our delusion.

On a cosmic scale, the experiences of the six classes of beings in the three realms of existence (the desire, form, and formless realms)—the whole of cyclic existence—are collective dramas unfolding as expressions of their group karma. When we see a movie projected on a screen, we invest it with a certain degree of reality, and for that reason are affected by it. We become upset, overjoyed, terrified, or angered by what we see, even if we understand how film works. A movie changes us by evoking particular emotional states. We might step back and say that, ultimately speaking, there is nothing there; it's just a movie. But for the most part we remain totally absorbed in the experience. If a group of people sit in front of the same movie screen, they will be affected in more or less the same way. A comedy will make them happy; a horror movie will scare them. As human beings sharing collective karma within the desire realm, we find that the strongest impulses in our minds are desire and attachment, which shape our common perceptions of reality.

Although great meditators can glimpse other realms of experience, we have no absolute proof that any realm, including our human world, exists beyond our individual and collective minds. Still, just as we take our dreams to be real while we sleep, we hold the human realm to be real. And the five other realms are as real to the beings who dwell in them as our experience is to us. Ultimately, suffering comes not from the phenomena of those realms, but from the fact that beings invest them with reality.

Thus, it is not contradictory to say that our experience is real or true and at the same time false. Nor is it contradictory to say the same about any other realm. If we insist that the human realm is real, then all the other realms are real because the beings in them experience them as real.

The most acute suffering in all the realms is that of the eighteen hells, the reflection and karmic consequence of anger and hatred and the thoughts, words, and actions arising from them. Hell beings suffer from extreme heat or cold. In the hot hells, flames the length of one's forearm cover the entire surface. With each step one's foot burns. When it's raised, it heals; then with the next step, it burns again. The fire blazes with an inconceivable intensity. Flames produced by burning pure sandalwood are said to be seven times hotter than ordinary fire, and seven times hotter still is the fire that will consume the universe at the end of this age. But the fire of the hot hells is seven times hotter than even that.

The bodies of hell beings are not the same as ours. Our flesh-and-blood body has a certain level of tolerance; it can stand or feel only so much pain. But hell beings, whose bodies are as sensitive as our eyeball, do not faint, lose consciousness, or die until their karma is finished.

In one hell, images of whomever one has killed—whether a deer, an insect, or a person—loom as large as mountains and one is crushed between them. As they separate, one's body becomes whole once more, only to be crushed again, and so on indefinitely. In another hell, beings are born with a line running the length of their bodies along which they're sawed in half. The two halves grow together, only to be cut through again, and so on.

In the cold hells, beings suffer without clothing or shelter in a frozen, desolate, and brutal environment. Whereas we humans fall asleep and die when we freeze, beings in this bone-cold realm, no matter how frozen they become, don't die until their karma is exhausted. Their bodies crack like meat left too long in a freezer.

Hundreds of times more horrific than any other realm, hell is quite simply the worst place to be.

Hungry ghosts suffer from intense hunger, thirst, and exposure to the elements. Again, this realm is not simply a metaphor, but very real to the beings trapped there, starving and burning with thirst. The very structure of their bodies creates pain. They have enormous heads, huge as mountains, and stomachs the size of valleys. Their necks are as narrow as a horsehair, so nothing can get through their gullets. Their limbs are so emaciated that they can't support themselves, and it is extremely difficult for them to get around to search for food. For the most part, hungry ghosts can only lie prone and starve. If they do find food, it is usually filthy or putrid and turns to fire in their bellies if they manage to swallow it.

Extreme greed and attachment are the karmic causes of rebirth in the hungry ghost realm. As long as the karma sustaining their existence has not been exhausted, hungry ghosts are unable to die despite their agony, which may continue for thousands of years.

In the animal realm, suffering results primarily from the predation of one species on another. Animals live in perpetual fear of their predators or competitors. Wild animals don't eat a single mouthful of grass without maintaining constant vigilance. The harsh treatment of animals domesticated by humans also causes great pain and suffering. Animals have very limited freedom; no matter how big and powerful the elephant or how pretty the peacock, neither has the ability to think something through and then act. This karma results from nonvirtuous actions motivated by ignorance and stupidity.

Virtuous actions stained by all the mind's poisons, with no one poison predominating, produce rebirth as a human being.

Though the conditions in this realm are relatively fortunate, nonetheless humans know the suffering of birth, old age, sickness, and death, of war, violence, famine, and unfulfilled desire.

Demigods have a pleasant environment, but they are plagued by jealousy and competitiveness and so are always engaged in strife, bloodshed, and warfare. Rebirth as a demigod is the result of virtuous actions stained by jealousy and rivalry, by doing something helpful only to prove one's superior qualities or activities.

In the worldly god realm, the karma of virtue stained by pride produces very wonderful conditions. Worldly gods never get dirty, never smell, never have to wash their clothes. The flowers that adorn their bodies stay fresh forever. Seven days before they die, however, their flowers decay, their bodies get dirty and begin to smell, and they suffer, knowing death is near. For seven days—the equivalent of three hundred and fifty human years—they endure the anguish of knowing which lower realm they're going to fall into. Finally, when the karma sustaining their existence is exhausted, god realm beings die.

Gods in the form and formless realms experience a kind of crude *samadhi,* or meditative absorption. Formless realm rebirth is produced by attachment to meditative stability, form realm rebirth by attachment to clarity, and desire god realm rebirth by attachment to bliss. Though not terrible, these rebirths still fall within samsara. Sooner or later, once the positive karma sustaining them is exhausted, the gods' intoxication will end and they will be reborn in a lower realm of greater suffering.

Once aware of the suffering and the limitations of cyclic existence, we become motivated to find a way out, just as when we realize we're sick, we seek medicine. Understanding that virtue and nonvirtue determine whether our experience is one of happiness or sorrow, pleasure or pain, we are left with a choice: we can either change our habits and develop virtuous qualities, seeking liberation for ourselves and all beings, or we can continue to create nonvirtue, perpetuating endless suffering.

When we really start to understand suffering, we begin to see samsara as a rotting swamp we've all fallen into. We desire only to free ourselves and others. That attitude of turning away from the causes of suffering and turning toward the causes of our own and others' liberation is called *renunciation,* a critical element of our entry into the spiritual path.

Through continuous contemplation of our precious human existence, death and impermanence, karma, and suffering, our mind turns toward the dharma. If you can see through the three poisons that fuel samsara so that they no longer hold sway in your mind, then you have successfully contemplated the four thoughts. If not, keep reflecting on them until they're part of you, until they have transformed your view of the world.

QUESTION: During practice, I sometimes experience deep longing or sadness. Is this the all-pervasive suffering described in Buddhist teachings, and if so, how can I dispel it?

RESPONSE: To feel sadness or longing in practice is not necessarily a bad thing. If it reflects a sincere sorrow and disgust for samsara based on an understanding of the limitations of ordinary existence, it may be beneficial—but only if it inspires us to do something about suffering. If we just indulge in the sadness and don't exert ourselves in practice so that we can eliminate the causes of suffering for ourselves and others, then it won't be of much use.

QUESTION: I find that when I'm in a lot of pain, it's very hard to contemplate the suffering of others.

RESPONSE: It may seem difficult, but thinking deeply about the suffering of others is the most effective way to deal with your own. It takes your mind off yourself and, more important, brings forth compassion. Compassion is very powerful, because it helps to purify the karma that produced the pain you feel. When that karma is completely purified, your suffering will naturally cease.

Contemplating suffering inspires us to look for ways to bring it to an end, both for ourselves and for others. That is why the first of the four noble truths taught by the Buddha was the truth of suffering. Happiness can actually be an obstacle to practice, because it robs us of our motivation to change. On the other hand, the more we contemplate and understand the character and causes of suffering, the more diligently we will apply spiritual methods to change it. The swiftest way to do so is to gain insight into the true nature of suffering itself—not just intellectually, but experientially.

12

How to Contemplate
the Four Thoughts

EACH OF US IS LIKE someone standing on the edge of a crumbling cliff, the earth rapidly breaking away. Telling ourselves, "I'm too hot, too tired, too sick, too busy to do my practice" is like saying we can't make the effort to run away from the ground eroding beneath our feet. It means we don't understand the four thoughts. Once we fully comprehend them, we'll realize the necessity of jumping to safety. What's more, when we see someone else close to the edge and about to fall, we'll rush to help; we won't claim we're too tired or busy.

To arrive at this understanding, we need to reflect on the four thoughts, to examine them critically, to ask ourselves, "Is it true that I have no alternative but the practice of dharma to break out of the unending cycles of existence?" Through repeated contemplation, sometimes called analytical meditation, we can change our deeply ingrained thought patterns. If we didn't contemplate, the same old mental poisons—ignorance, attachment, aversion, jealousy, and pride—would come up day after day, year after year. Simply trying to quiet the mind isn't enough to overcome them. That's like pushing the "pause" button on a tape recorder so we won't have to listen to music we don't like. For as long as we hold the button, we don't hear anything, but the moment we release it, the music we so dislike starts playing again. In contemplation, we do more than interrupt the tape—we erase it and make a new recording. We transform our ordinary habits of mind, as well as negative thoughts and actions. Then we hear a different sound, one far more harmonious and beneficial.

The ordinary mind is like a legless man, while the winds, or subtle energies, of the body are like a blind wild horse. This combination is what can make meditation so difficult. In our practice, therefore, we address both aspects of the mind—its knowing quality and its quality of movement.

Taming the mind is similar to taming a wild horse. We don't restrain it tightly with a short tether, which might frighten it and cause it to hurt itself trying to get free. Instead, we let it run in a very large corral. It is not really free, but it doesn't feel confined, because it has freedom of movement. As we spend more time with the horse, as it gets to know and trust us, it slowly loses some of its fear and allows us to come closer. As it begins to calm down, we can gradually make the corral smaller.

When we want to tame the mind, we shouldn't try to restrain it at first. Instead of allowing thoughts to run wild, we make a large corral of virtue by transforming negative concepts into positive ones. The mind isn't really free, yet it isn't completely confined. This way, we work with mind's qualities of movement, its unceasing display.

In addition to analytical meditation, we practice in a more nonconceptual way, simply letting the mind relax and fall into its natural state, without any contemplation. Here we cut the mind's attachment to concepts, its habit of always thinking of past or future, likes and dislikes—as if constantly stirring the water in a muddy pond, never letting it settle and clarify. In so doing, we work with mind's self-knowing quality.

In this way, we utilize two principles of Buddhist practice. The nonconceptual technique is called *shamatha* in Sanskrit or *zhinay* in Tibetan. *Zhi* means "to pacify obscurations" and *nay* "to maintain," so "zhinay" refers to the calm, tranquil abiding in which discursive and distracting thought patterns are pacified and the mind comes to rest one-pointedly.

The contemplative technique, using the rational mind in a skillful, inquiring way, is called *vipashyana* in Sanskrit or *lhagtong* in Tibetan, which means "deeper insight," seeing beyond ordinary seeing. Together, shamatha and vipashyana are like the handle and blade of a sword with which we cut through our holding to the apparent solidity of our subject–object experience. We sever the tight bonds of attachment, ego clinging, and self-interest, thus conquering afflictive emotions and ignorance.

In employing both methods, we work toward resolving duality by cutting attachment not only to ordinary thoughts, but also to nonconceptual, blissful, or extraordinary meditation experiences. We thereby cut the roots of the grosser reflection of the mind's poisons—samsara—as well as the subtler reflection of the mind's positive qualities—nirvana. When we alternate these two methods, slowly and subtly our perspective begins to change. What starts as intellectual understanding gradually becomes more personal and experiential. We approach the true nature of mind beyond the extremes of "is" and "isn't," thought and no-thought.

To attain enlightenment, we need both shamatha and vipashyana; neither by itself is sufficient. A bird needs both wings to fly—we need both method and wisdom, contemplation and relaxation. If we're tempted to believe that we can attain enlightenment or even happiness by simply thinking, we need only remind ourselves that we've been thinking from beginningless time, so much so that our ideas could fill volumes. Yet no matter how methodical or intelligent, our thinking hasn't made us any happier; it certainly hasn't led us to enlightenment. If thinking alone produced enlightenment, we would already be buddhas.

On the other hand, a blank mind doesn't produce enlightenment either. Bears and prairie dogs hibernate for months at a time, yet their state of blankness doesn't produce enlightenment. Attachment to meditative stability can lead to a blissful existence for eons in a formless realm in which there is neither thought nor a physical body. Once the karma sustaining that existence is exhausted, however, the mindstream falls into a lower realm to suffer once again.

Allowing the mind to rest is effortless and reveals an indwelling, nondual awareness that does not involve a subject being aware of an object. Usually, when people meditate, they try to *do* something. But instead of trying, simply let the mind relax and rest in the free and spontaneously open space in which thoughts arise and subside. Thoughts of past, present, and future will naturally occur, but don't grasp at, follow, suppress, or push them away. When thoughts arise, they almost invariably stem from ignorance, attachment, or aversion. Their recurrence in the mindstream forms the basis for the continuity of samsara, so instead of being upset when they come up, respond to them with compassion, realizing that this is how you and all other beings become caught in suffering. Thinking, "There's a thought—I have to get rid of it" is like the pot calling the kettle black, for both are thoughts. The goal is neither to think nor not to think, but rather to reveal the essence of mind.

In the beginning, the mind won't stay relaxed for very long, because the habit of conceptualizing is so strong. Instead of getting caught up in ordinary thoughts, contemplate the persistence of the thought process itself and use it to turn the mind back to dharma. Redirect your ordinary thinking with the following step-by-step process.

Begin by contemplating one of the four thoughts, and then allow the mind to relax. Then pray to the lama, or another object of your faith, for the blessing to accomplish something of benefit for yourself and others before impermanence intervenes and you no longer have this body. Arouse compassion for the predicament of beings and make the wish that all will be liberated from the cycles of suffering. Then establish the commitment to apply your understanding and the methods of dharma diligently in order to accomplish this. Then contemplate the next thought, again allow the mind to rest, then pray, arouse compassion, and confirm your commitment to free all beings from suffering, and so forth. In following this process, you will come closer to a direct experience of mind's nature, the absolute truth that cannot be grasped through words or concepts.

Meditating like this will prevent our practice from stagnating, the way milk forms a film when left in an open dish. We keep it fresh at each step. The key to meditation lies in cutting: after contemplating, we cut our attachment to concepts by relaxing. Then we cut our attachment to relaxation in order to pray. We pray, then we cut; we develop compassion and cut; we reestablish our commitment and cut to the next thought. This way, the mind won't fall into ordinary thinking, and we'll stay alert and focused in the quick of the experience. Meditation becomes fresher as it moves, like a stream as it tumbles against one rock and then another so that by the time it reaches the bottom of the cascade, it is very pure.

Awareness of mind's true nature and the thinking process are not mutually exclusive. Rather, they are inseparable—a good practitioner never loses awareness while eating, driving to work, or playing with children. The real skill in meditation lies in not losing awareness in the moment of transition from one thought or activity to another. By being fully present with each experience and each transition, you remain close to their essence. It's like riding a wave. You become one with the movement of the wave as it rises and falls. If you get ahead of, behind, or separated from it, you fall—you lose it. In this way, you can learn how to ride the wave of the thinking process while not losing awareness.

The Sutra of the Bodhisattva Essence of Space contains a dialogue between a bodhisattva, Namkhai Nyingpo, and the Buddha Shakyamuni. The bodhisattva asks, "What is the spiritual meaning of leisure and opportunity?" The Buddha replies, "When the mind is distracted by discursive thought, there is busyness and activity. When the mind experiences peace due to the calming of discursive thought and the subsiding of that thought into the basic space of mind, there is leisure."

In addition to the outer sense of leisure—having the opportunity to practice—there exists this inner sense, the unique human potential to experience the natural relaxation of the mind, the falling away of discursive thought. Until we know leisure in the inner sense, our dharma practice won't be very effective, because we will be perpetually distracted by thoughts and concepts.

Another method for deepening our understanding of the four thoughts involves visualization. Begin by establishing pure motivation, your aspiration to attain enlightenment in order to help beings go beyond suffering and find permanent bliss and happiness. Then, in as much detail as you can, think about how things change. When your mind becomes weary, relax. Don't force it; true relaxation doesn't last very long at first.

When thoughts begin surfacing again, visualize yourself in very high, rugged terrain where sheer black rock cliffs rise precipitously. You have nothing to cling to. Only one precarious path snakes along the steep sides of the cliff, becoming progressively narrower until it completely disappears. Snarling, ravenous beasts are chasing you, but you've got nowhere to run. They close in; there is no safety anywhere. You're helpless, without friends or family, without hope.

In desperation, you call upon your teacher, God, or Buddha—someone or something greater than you, and infallible. That embodiment of perfection appears, saying, "Don't be afraid. These treacherous black cliffs have arisen as the result of your clinging from beginningless time to a belief in the truth of ordinary reality. This belief has become so strong that great danger surrounds you. Ignorance makes the landscape dark. These beasts that mean to kill you represent ripening karma you've created with your own poisonous mind. This narrow path that disappears into nothingness is the way of samsara. Whatever has come together will separate; whatever is happening now will at some point cease. Day by day, each step you take will pass without any possibility of reclamation or control. The shortness of the path indicates the insufficiency of the karma sustaining your life."

Then the infallible being you have invoked asks, "What is death? What is samsara? It seems good, bad, happy, sad, but it's like a dream. There is not a trace in it of anything true or solid. Delusion and ignorance perpetuate phantom experiences of danger and terror. To awaken from this dream is to realize the birthless and deathless absolute nature."

After you have finished the visualization, let your mind rest. Finally, dedicate the merit of your practice to all beings, that they may awaken from the dream of suffering.

Through this meditation, you will see that delusion, ignorance, mental poisons, karma, and belief in the truth of an insubstantial reality all create the precarious conditions of cyclic existence. By recognizing impermanence and contemplating the empty, dreamlike nature of your experience, you will undermine your belief in its solidity.

Meditation on the four thoughts brings maturity to our spiritual path. Without it, we merely have "fair weather practice." There is a Tibetan saying: as long as our food tastes delicious, our clothing is warm, the sun shines, and everything seems to be going fine, our practice will be reliable. But as soon as something goes wrong, a friend turns on us, we lose something or someone dear, it goes out the window. It doesn't support us in times of need or provide refuge from pain and fear.

Our practice needs to be stronger—and to work more swiftly—than our obscurations. To control an old-fashioned bicycle we're riding downhill, we have to pedal very quickly. In the same way, we have to work fast to avert the rapidly spinning negativities that are quickly taking us downhill. Otherwise, our anger, desire, and ignorance will only become more deeply ingrained.

Body, speech, and mind and the precious opportunity they offer are no more lasting or real than a bubble, no more permanent or substantial than a dream. We have to seize the moment, before it's lost and impermanence takes its toll.

QUESTION: If I'm meditating and I start to experience love or bliss, am I supposed to squelch it? Is this the same as cutting?

RESPONSE: You don't have to try to get rid of bliss. But when your mind turns to compassion, bliss naturally dissolves. Bliss, clarity, and stability are natural by-products of meditation, but they can become obstacles to meditation and to the path of enlightenment if we get attached to them. So cutting is crucial.

Once a large caravan was traveling on pilgrimage from eastern to central Tibet. Because of the threat posed by thieves and wild animals, people took turns watching the herd of yaks. One day, as they prepared to break camp, the group discovered that the monk who had stood watch the night before was missing. They searched for him high and low for several days but could find no sign of him, not even a shred of clothing.

Finally, they reluctantly moved on and, assuming him dead, made offerings on his behalf at all the monasteries on their pilgrimage. Several months later, one of the lamas to whom they made offerings and requested prayers declined their offerings, saying that prayer was unnecessary since nothing had happened to the monk. The astonished pilgrims insisted that he must be dead, for he couldn't have survived so long without food or shelter. But the lama told them exactly how to find the monk, assuring them that he would be fine if they continued their pilgrimage and looked for him on the way home.

On their return to the old campsite, they followed the lama's instructions and found the monk sitting in meditation under a grassy outcropping. Shaken from his meditative state, he immediately asked, "Where are the yaks?" He had been in a trance-like state for months, unaware that his companions had gone, unaware of his surroundings, yet his mind hadn't changed at all. Attachment to states like this doesn't produce enlightenment—only rebirth in a formless realm.

Smoke and sparks are signs that a fire is burning, but they are not the purpose of the fire; bliss, clarity, and stability are signs of meditation, but they are not its goal. They won't bring us any closer to liberation.

QUESTION: What about visionary experiences caused by mind-altering substances?

RESPONSE: They don't count. What we're talking about are meditational experiences, not those induced by drugs. It's not wise to use any mind-altering substances, because in doing so you relinquish the power of your mind. With drug use you will establish a karmic pattern in which you have little or no control over your mind. In your next rebirth, you may be mentally retarded or very unstable; you may even be born as an animal.

Once someone offered me some LSD. My wife, Jane, discouraged me from using it, but I wanted to see for myself what so many people were experiencing. At the time, my liver was quite weak; when I ingested the substance, I felt terrible pain and lost consciousness. When I came to, I had visions, but they were obviously only the display of my ordinary mind's concepts. None of them had any deep meaning, much to the dismay of the students who had come with notebooks and pens to observe and record my experience. Visions that arise in meditation as the display of mind's pure nature are far clearer and more beautiful.

QUESTION: Some practitioners seem to have a strong interest in the Buddhist teachings, but at the same time are resistant to them. Will contemplating the four thoughts help them? What else can they do?

RESPONSE: There is no simple answer. Resistance to the dharma can arise for different reasons. Some people are initially interested in the teachings, find them very helpful, and begin to practice. But at a certain point, something goes awry and they end up holding an extremely negative view of the dharma. In many cases, this can be attributed either to karma created in past lifetimes or to conditions and circumstances in this lifetime, such as a hindering or demonic force that influences the mind and creates doubts. Ideally, a person who wants to practice but feels resistant to doing so should consult a master with the ability to see beyond the surface of things in order to determine what kind of ceremony, practice, or other step would be useful.

QUESTION: Do the thoughts and emotions that come up in our dreams sow karmic seeds?

RESPONSE: For an action to have full karmic consequences, four elements must be present: the basis for action (the object); the motivation of the agent; the action itself; and its results. If one of these elements is missing, then the seriousness of the karmic consequences is diminished. But, even so, the action is not karmically neutral.

Although dreams are not as powerful as waking experiences in their capacity to generate karma, they nevertheless do so. As long as there is intention in the mind, some accumulation of karma results and it must be confessed and purified, whether or not it translates into actual words and deeds. We need to address the mind, because once we have eliminated negative intention, there will no longer be any basis for negative speech and actions.

QUESTION: So all of samsara is really full of suffering? How will understanding this help my practice?

RESPONSE: If you look closely at samsara, you will find that there is no lasting happiness anywhere, nothing to base your hope on. There aren't any samsaric circumstances you could create, no matter how great the virtue, that would produce lasting happiness.

People often squirm when they hear this; it makes them very uncomfortable. But we need to think about it until we realize that the spiritual path, difficult as it may be, is our only alternative.

If we travel the spiritual path diligently, if our practice is pure and strong, we can purify karma. We need to contemplate the four thoughts to inspire diligence, to ensure that we're not just making futile gestures or practicing a kind of false spirituality.

We wouldn't want to be like Tibetan moogoots, humanoid animals similar to the American Sasquatch or Bigfoot. Moogoots are shy and keep to themselves in the forest. Hiding among the trees, they watch the farmers till the ground. When the farmers go home for the night, the moogoots come out and mimic their activities. They don't know what they are doing, so they beat the ground, stomp on things, and generally do a lot of damage. What they don't do is farm. We don't want to follow their example, mimicking the actions of spiritual practitioners when all we're doing is thrashing around and wrecking things.

By thinking about the preciousness of the human body and impermanence, we cut through attachment to our worldly experience. When we understand that no matter where we're born in samsara, great difficulties will arise and that all happiness is temporary, we cut through our complacent belief that it's enough to be born in a higher realm. We begin to develop the unwavering intention to achieve enlightenment instead of settling for ordinary rebirth, which will only perpetuate our confusion.

Think, relax, pray, arouse compassion, renew your commitment. Pray to work ceaselessly to liberate all beings from the cycles of suffering. Pray to develop the ability to release all beings, wherever they are, into their true nature.

There was a very great practitioner in my family, Tulku Arig, one of my cherished teachers. People traveled hundreds of miles just to look at the place where he meditated. Even the Chinese Communists said, "If you practice dharma the way he does, it's okay." He owned only what he could carry on his back and lived in either a cave or small meditation cabin. His practice was pure and simple. From the age of thirteen until his passing at the age of eighty-four, he slept for only one hour a night because meditation was more important to him than sleep.

As a teacher he could be quite wrathful, directly confronting his students' attachments and aversions. When students came to him, for the first four years he taught nothing but the four thoughts. He insisted that they penetrate the meaning and understand the consequences of these teachings until their minds changed and their practice matured. When they begged Tulku Arig to give more profound teachings, he said, "This teaching may not be good enough for you, but it was good enough for the buddhas. They meditated for years in order to understand the truth of the four thoughts. If this teaching is not profound enough for you, go somewhere else."

If you really understand the four thoughts, then you can meditate. But don't think that meditation is a piece of cake. When the great yogi Milarepa was asked, "How hard is your practice?" he replied that it was harder than carrying salt from the lake beds. To transport salt in Tibet, one filled a wet yak skin with wet salt and pressed it until the skin bulged, then let it dry. The drying yak skin would squeeze the packed salt, turning it into a hard rock. Milarepa said it was easier to carry such rocks of salt up and down a mountain all day long than to meditate.

If we intend to go beyond karma and the cycles of suffering, we have to meditate with tremendous intensity throughout our lives. We need to understand beyond a doubt that there is no getting around karma, that there is no lasting happiness anywhere in samsara, that what we have right now is the greatest opportunity of all, and that it is short-lived.

It's as if we had fallen off a cliff, grasped a protruding branch, and were dangling in midair: we have no time to waste, no time for a coffee break. If we don't value this human opportunity, we won't use it before the branch gives way.

Don't deny the truth of the four thoughts. They may be hard to swallow, but don't fool yourself. Think about them. Contemplate them. Fathom what they mean and experience what they provide for meditation. They are called the supports to meditation, like the four posts of a platform you sit upon. They are transformative: they turn the mind toward the dharma, toward truth.

PART III

Refuge and Bodhicitta

13

Refuge

WE KNOW THAT OUR contemplation of the four thoughts has been effective if we begin to see through our samsaric experience, to understand that it lacks substance, that nothing within it is reliable or unchanging. What then can we count on? Where will we find true heart, true essence? Only in the sacred dharma will we discover something of absolute value.

The four thoughts fall into the category of introductory teachings called the *ordinary preliminaries,* common to all Buddhist traditions. Although foundational to the practice of dharma, contemplating them doesn't constitute a formal step in the Buddhist path. To go further, we need to make a commitment, embodied in the refuge vow. This is the first gate to Buddhist practice.

The word "refuge" denotes a place of safety or protection. In essence, the vow of refuge involves making a commitment to go the way of harmlessness. It's not that, once we take refuge, the Buddha or some other enlightened being waves a magic wand, delivering us from pain or dissatisfaction. Rather, we ensure our own protection by addressing the root of suffering, which lies in our own harmful thoughts and actions. If we reduce these through the disciplined use of body, speech, and mind, we avert their negative karmic consequences and thereby eliminate the causes of suffering.

The motivation for taking refuge in the Mahayana and Vajra-yana Buddhist traditions is selfless compassion for the limitless beings suffering in cyclic existence and a sincere desire to attain liberation in order to free them. The vow of refuge lasts not only for this lifetime but until we attain enlightenment, however far in the future that may be.

We take refuge in the Three Jewels—the Buddha, dharma, and sangha. The Buddha is one who has walked a certain road and, by virtue of having reached the destination, knows the route and can show us the way. The road itself is the dharma. And those with whom we travel, those who offer us support and on whom we rely, comprise the sangha. In taking refuge, we follow in the footsteps of those before us who have walked the path to enlightenment.

Taking refuge requires that we have an appreciation for the qualities of the Three Jewels, beginning with those of the infallible, enlightened Buddha. Many great saints and teachers have founded spiritual paths throughout the world, but they haven't possessed the attributes of the Buddha Shakyamuni. Having completely purified the afflictive emotions, karma, habit, and intellectual obscuration, the Buddha exhibited the thirty-two major and eighty minor marks of enlightened body, the sixty qualities of enlightened speech, and the two omniscient qualities of enlightened mind. His 112 marks of physical perfection—for example, a radiant aura or halo apparent to all and the fact that his feet didn't touch the ground—were a visible and unmistakable display of perfect realization. Those who came in contact with the Buddha were awestruck; they knew they had encountered an extraordinary being. He didn't have to proclaim himself a teacher—it was obvious.

That sixty melodious tones marked the Buddha's speech doesn't mean that he had a beautiful singing voice or was a good orator. Rather, his speech functioned as a perfect vehicle for communication. All of those who listened to a single teaching by the Buddha, no matter how vast the audience, heard perfectly, without amplification, a wealth of wisdom in their own language, as well as answers to their own particular questions.

The Buddha's mind was imbued with two kinds of knowledge: an omniscient, detailed, and discriminating awareness of phenomena on a conventional level and a profound awareness of the true nature of reality.

In acknowledging these qualities, we recognize the Buddha as an infallible teacher who for countless eons practiced harmlessness and helpfulness, purified karma, accumulated merit and wisdom, and thus attained the goal of enlightenment. The Buddha, like a raw diamond, underwent the process of being cut, ground, and polished, becoming a brilliant, perfectly finished gem. Though we have the same potential, the rest of us are still rough diamonds, our perfect qualities obscured.

In taking refuge, we rely on the Buddha's example because, having accomplished the path, he has shown us the way. If we had to traverse a hazardous swamp, someone who had successfully completed the journey, who knew exactly where to go and what to avoid, would be a supremely valuable guide. The Buddha is such a guide. He has shown us what to abandon and what to embrace, pointing out the direction to take and demonstrating every step on the path to enlightenment.

Second, we take refuge in the sacred dharma: the teachings of the Buddha and the methods he gave us for achieving enlightenment—a great multiplicity of means, complete and without error, which are his legacy. Here everything is clearly spelled out: the foundation, path, and fruition of practice, how to begin, overcome hindrances, and enrich the positive qualities that begin to develop. These methods are generally divided into nine categories, or *yanas* (Sanskrit for "vehicles"), comprising three basic approaches: the Hinayana path of personal salvation, the Mahayana path of those seeking liberation for all beings, and the Vajrayana teachings within the Mahayana, often referred to as the short path.

Third, we take refuge in the sangha, the many practitioners who have applied the Buddha's methods and maintained his legacy in an unbroken oral lineage, preserving the scriptures that enshrine the teachings, and in the mind-to-mind lineage, a vibrant tradition of personal experience that reveals the truth of these teachings. Because every generation since the Buddha has produced individuals devoted to realizing the teachings, the dharma has not become dry and intellectual but remains fresh and alive. The sangha is like a living *mala,* or strand of prayer beads—practitioners connected by their practice through the centuries, exemplifying the teachings and maintaining a vital tradition that is accessible to us today and will continue to be so for generations to come.

Thus the Three Jewels are an infallible source of refuge from our suffering, ignorance, and confusion. Such refuge cannot be provided by anything impermanent or anyone still bound by conditioned existence—no matter how famous, appealing, powerful, wealthy, or influential.

Refuge, like many other aspects of the dharma, has three levels of meaning. We have already discussed its outer significance. It also has inner and secret meanings.

In the Vajrayana tradition, the inner sources of refuge are the Three Roots—the lama, yidam, and dakini. They are said to be the source of blessings, spiritual accomplishment, and enlightened activity, respectively.

The lama, or spiritual teacher, is the root of blessings in that she imparts the knowledge, methods, and wisdom that enable us to achieve liberation. The yidam, or chosen meditation deity, is the root of accomplishment in that, through practice relying on the deity, we are able to realize the nature of mind. We also realize the dakini, the feminine principle of wisdom, from which arises the accomplishment of enlightened activity.

The secret object of refuge is none other than the true nature of mind, faultless buddha nature—the essence of every being, whether god, human, animal, hungry ghost, or hell being. This nature has two facets: the first, *dharmakaya,* the absolute nature of mind beyond ordinary concepts, can be likened to the sun; the second, *rupakaya,* or form kaya, can be likened to the sun's brilliant radiance, which occurs naturally and without effort. This radiance, manifesting for the benefit of others, has two aspects: the *sambhogakaya,* the pure form manifestation perceptible to great practitioners; and the *nirmanakaya* manifestation that arises for the benefit of those unable to perceive the sambhogakaya expression.

In Vajrayana Buddhism, by relying on outer, inner, and secret objects of refuge, we purify karma on outer, inner, and secret levels simultaneously. It's like cutting with three blades instead of one.

Our endless experience of samsaric suffering is analogous to that of a fly caught in a capped milk bottle. To try to escape, it may fly up, down, and all around, to no avail. Taking refuge with the goal of attaining enlightenment to benefit all beings is like removing the cap from the bottle. Although the fly may not find the opening to freedom immediately, it eventually will. Once we take refuge, we can be sure that our suffering in samsara will eventually end.

However, having taken refuge, we can't just sit back and wait for the Three Jewels to bless us. If we don't do any work to ripen our mind, we won't be receptive to their blessings. Taking refuge involves making a personal commitment. It's not a casual thing to be treated lightly, not something we change our mind about somewhere down the line. We are often indecisive about our spiritual path. We keep waffling, thinking that first one thing, then another, will work, rarely committing ourselves, and never really getting anywhere.

Suppose we wanted to reach a mountaintop and could follow a number of paths to get there. If we took a few steps up one path, then thought another might be better and tried it for a few steps, then decided a third would get us there faster, continuing indefinitely in that fashion, we would never get to the top. We would only circle around. When we take refuge, we make a personal decision about which path is right for us and a commitment to follow that path.

The idea of undertaking this commitment sometimes makes people apprehensive. Yet such apprehension is like the fear of using an antidote after having swallowed poison. The time for doubt is before swallowing, not after. Taking refuge simply means accepting the fact that you have ingested poison and deciding to take the necessary medicine. It means saying to yourself, "This is it for me. I am committed to not harming others. That is definite. I am committed to working for the benefit of others, and not merely for myself. I am certain about that. Until now I haven't paid much attention to my mind or examined its nature or the way it works. But from now on I will be mindful and alert; I'll keep a firm watch. I will make an effort to accentuate and encourage what is virtuous in me and to reverse and eventually eliminate my nonvirtuous tendencies." Only that kind of unshakable commitment makes the vow of refuge effective.

The benefits of taking refuge in this way are truly incalculable. One of the Buddhist scriptures states that if these benefits had tangible form, they would be larger than the entire three-thousand-fold universe. This is not insignificant, for the term "three-thousand-fold universe" refers to a billion world systems (1,000 × 1,000 × 1,000). Through the blessings of our sources of refuge, we receive guidance, methods, and support for our spiritual practice and for achieving ultimate liberation. When our efforts meet these blessings, we can awaken to our intrinsic awareness, the true nature of mind. This is what it means to take refuge in the deepest sense.

QUESTION: Once you are enlightened, can you ever go back? Are there stages to enlightenment or enlightenment experiences?

RESPONSE: There is really no such thing as an enlightenment experience. I've heard many people refer to this idea, but they don't really understand the meaning of liberation. To attain enlightenment we need to purify the four obscurations—the poisons of the mind, intellectual obscuration, karma, and habit—and establish fortunate conditions through the accumulation of merit. Those who have done so manifest unmistakable qualities and create two kinds of benefit. The first, benefit for oneself—the removal of all obscurations and the recognition of one's intrinsic nature—is the realization of dharmakaya. This realization liberates us from ignorance, and freedom from ignorance liberates us from the consequences of ignorance. The second, benefit for others, is the realization of the two form kayas, which are like the warmth and light given off naturally by the sunlike dharmakaya.

Once a woman addressing a panel I was on said that, three years before, she had been in a car accident. She felt she had become enlightened at that time and asked if we thought this was possible. Each panelist deferred to the next, until finally I questioned her, "Do you have anger?"

"Yes," she replied.

"Do you have desire?"

Again she said, "Yes."

"Then," I told her, "you aren't enlightened."

In the course of meditation practice, one may mistake experiences of bliss, clarity, and stability for enlightenment. But the qualities of enlightenment are truly different and unmistakable. One is no longer bound by samsaric mind or samsaric existence, and there is no possibility of losing that realization.

QUESTION: What is the difference between making a commitment by formally taking refuge and simply not harming? Why is the formal commitment important?

RESPONSE: Suppose you make a commitment never to kill a dragon. Most people will never see a dragon in their entire lives; some think dragons don't exist. So, you might ask, why would anyone make a commitment not to kill a dragon?

If you never kill a dragon, you aren't creating any nonvirtue, yet at the same time you're not creating any virtue. From the day you make a commitment not to kill a dragon, and continue to uphold that commitment, you're accumulating virtue. In taking refuge, you accumulate great virtue minute by minute as you uphold your vows.

QUESTION: What are the 84,000 methods of the Buddhadharma?

RESPONSE: In India, the Buddha Shakyamuni taught the Tripitaka—the Three Collections of the Dharma. The Vinaya primarily addresses desire; the Sutra teachings mainly concern antidotes to anger; and the Abhidharma addresses ignorance. Each of these consist of 21,000 methods. Later, the Buddha taught the Vajrayana, in which he introduced an additional 21,000 methods for removing all the mind's obscurations.

The teachings in these collections were brought to Tibet and translated. All of the Buddha's spoken words, which fill a hundred large volumes, remain accessible to us today.

QUESTION: The qualities of the precious sangha are sometimes more difficult to see than those of the Buddha and the dharma. It is often hard to maintain pure view of our peers. How does establishing a good relationship with fellow practitioners benefit our practice?

RESPONSE: To begin with, human existence is very rare, for other beings far outnumber humans. Further, of the hundreds of millions of beings within the human realm, how many actively pursue a path of virtue and benefit for others through their thoughts, words, and actions? How many try to avoid harming others and acting in nonvirtuous ways? The number of such people can be likened to the number of stars one can see in the daytime—very few indeed.

The Tibetan word for the Sanskrit *sangha* is *gedun,* which refers to someone who yearns for or is motivated by virtue. If people wish to create virtue, their motivation and personal commitment make them very special, even though they may not be flawless. Members of the Mahayana sangha vow to free not only themselves but all others from cyclic existence. How could we not revere that commitment as the best of all qualities? How could we focus instead on personal, temporary shortcomings? Those in the sangha are our companions until we attain enlightenment. Viewing them with respect and appreciation benefits us because it increases our merit. It purifies our negative habits and our negative karma.

QUESTION: Is it possible to take refuge in more than one spiritual tradition?

RESPONSE: We might think that by piecing together different spiritual paths, we can improve on existing traditions. People in the West are very creative. They know that a bicycle, car, train, or airplane will get them to their destination, but many would prefer to design their own custom vehicle by combining the wing of an airplane, the wheel of a car, and another part from a train or bicycle. Such a vehicle may or may not get them where they want to go. It might even be the cause of their death.

I find it difficult to imagine creating a spiritual vehicle pieced together from many traditions that would produce the same swift results as an established tradition like that of the Buddha—an enlightened being who purified all obscurations and who had boundless wisdom and compassion and the ability to benefit others. When you rely on an ancient spiritual tradition, you can be confident that by practicing as others did before you, you will achieve the same results.

It is difficult to recover from a serious illness without relying on an experienced, well-trained doctor and medicines that have proved effective for many people in the past. The illness of samsaric existence is complicated; it is not easy to cure and requires proven spiritual methods.

Before choosing a spiritual path, it may be useful to explore different traditions to decide where you feel a connection. Then you can apply the methods of a particular tradition to determine whether they are effective for you. If you find that your mind becomes less negative and your positive qualities increase, practicing that path will benefit you. The process is similar to reading a menu: you can try to guess what would taste best, but you won't know until you actually sample it.

Once you choose a spiritual path, it is very important to stick to it. Going from one tradition to another will only create confusion and instability. However, after establishing a firm foundation in one tradition, receiving teachings elsewhere from time to time may enhance your understanding of and appreciation for your own path.

QUESTION: Doesn't it seem sectarian to take refuge in only one tradition?

RESPONSE: "Nonsectarian" connotes an open mind, with respect for all traditions. However, this doesn't imply that we need to practice all paths, or many paths. Some people are confused about this; they think that being nonsectarian means assembling a mish-mash of methods from different traditions. Rather, each spiritual tradition should be honored and practiced with integrity.

People often make the mistake of finding fault with other traditions. But any tradition that champions virtue and deplores nonvirtue will benefit those who practice it, and so deserves our respect. Though they are different terms, the English "sun," Tibetan "nyima," and Sanskrit "surya" refer to exactly the same source of light and warmth. In the same way, any source of refuge that embodies wisdom and compassion will benefit those who rely on it.

The goal of all spiritual paths is fulfilled when beings are liberated from suffering. In the United States, we enjoy a great variety of restaurants—Japanese, Indian, Mexican, even Tibetan. Each of us can eat what we like—why denigrate others' choices? The important thing is that everyone eat. Similarly, why belittle others' spiritual choices? What matters is that we obtain spiritual nourishment through spiritual practice, for without it we will only experience greater suffering now and in future lives.

14

Giving Rise to Bodhicitta

IN ORDER TO DIRECT ourselves along the spiritual path, we
need a goal to work toward, as an arrow needs a target. With
bodhicitta, the next gate to practice in the Mahayana and Vajrayana traditions, we aim at enlightenment for the benefit of others
in every moment. This is the best of all possible goals.

Bodhicitta is foundational to all we do, like the root of a
medicinal tree whose branches, leaves, and flowers all produce
life-enhancing medicine. The quality and purity of our practice
depend on its permeating every method we use. With it, everything
is ensured. Without it, nothing will work.

This is why from the very first time we listen to the teachings
we are told to establish the liberation of all beings as the purpose
of our practice. We render ourselves fit vessels for spiritual teachings and practice by changing our motivation from one of self-
interest to one of altruism.

Bodhicitta has three components: arousing compassion for
the suffering of beings; aspiring to attain enlightenment in order
to benefit all beings, called *wishing bodhicitta;* and actively
engaging in the path of liberation in order to accomplish that
goal, called *engaging bodhicitta.*

The Tibetan term for the Sanskrit *bodhicitta* is *jang chub sem.*
Jang means the removal of obscurations; *chub,* the revealing of

all perfect qualities within, and *sem,* mind. Through the practice of bodhicitta, we purify obscurations and enhance our intrinsic positive qualities, revealing enlightened mind.

We can compare mind's obscurations to the clay covering a crystal that has long been in the ground. If we pick up the encrusted crystal, it looks like a clay ball. Yet its essential qualities are in no way reduced; they are only obscured. If we wash away the clay, the crystal becomes clear, its qualities apparent. In the same way, by purifying and removing the mind's obscurations, we reveal our true crystalline nature.

Though it lies within, we always look outside for this nature. It's like searching everywhere for a missing horse, following countless hoof prints through the forest, only to discover, finally, that the horse has never left the stable.

Compassion, the first aspect of bodhicitta, is also inherent within us. Although we naturally have good heart, it is usually rather limited. Through practice, we can expose and awaken our own perfect, boundless compassion.

Jang chub sem is thus both a method and the fruit of practice. Due to the momentum of bodhicitta, the sunlike essence of mind becomes completely revealed and benefit for others arises spontaneously and effortlessly, like the sun's reflection in every vessel and body of water.

We begin the practice of removing mind's obscurations by reducing our self-centeredness and redirecting our attention to others. Our habit of focusing on ourselves has been reinforced for countless lifetimes, which is why we're trapped in samsara. Buddhas have eliminated selfish and ordinary thoughts, developed selfless motivation, and thus achieved enlightenment.

The development of this kind of motivation rests on four cornerstones called the *four immeasurable qualities*. The first is equanimity, an attitude of equal regard toward all beings. If we can live free of prejudice or bias, without making a distinction between friends and enemies, then we have grasped the essence of existence and planted the seeds of our own and others' happiness and freedom.

Right now our love and compassion extend only to certain people, our family, friends, and loved ones, but not to those we perceive as enemies. We may not wish ill fortune on unpleasant or dangerous people, yet we might have trouble not rejoicing if something bad happens to them. Or our compassion for a sick child may derive simply from our attachment to her. Through the practice of equanimity, we develop a noble attitude of compassion for all beings without distinction, from the depths of our heart. Unless we have this kind of pure heart, our practice will remain superficial—we won't truly understand the purpose of dharma.

We develop equanimity, first, by realizing that all beings, equally, want happiness. Nobody wants to suffer. Second, we contemplate the fact that every being, at one time or another through countless lifetimes, has been our own mother. The Buddha Shakyamuni and other buddhas and bodhisattvas, who revealed the crystalline nature of their minds and became omniscient, taught that there is not one being who has not been our parent. This is something we too could perceive if we purified our mindstreams. Each being—no matter how antagonistic to us now—has been as kind and essential to us as our parents in this lifetime. A person who now plays a seemingly insignificant or even threatening role in our personal drama was once loving and helpful.

To develop an appreciation for this kindness, we need to recognize the enormous generosity of our parents. First and foremost, they gave us the gift of a human body. Upon death in our last incarnation, when our mind was plunged into the bardo, the frightening and chaotic intermediate state between death and rebirth, we were blown about helplessly, like a feather in the wind, without any stable frame of reference or support, experiencing terrifying sights and sounds. We finally found safety in our mother's womb at the moment of conception. From then on, our mother carried us in her body for nine months, putting up with discomfort and perhaps illness to give us our human birth.

When we were helpless in our cradle, our mother provided care and protection so that we could grow strong and healthy. Had she not nurtured us, or asked another to do so, we would surely have died.

She saved our young life again and again, protecting us from falling, from eating things that would make us sick, from coming too close to fire, water, traffic. She fed and clothed us, washed us, and kept our home clean. Think how much we would have to pay now for someone to clean our house or cook our meals. These days, when someone gives us a cup of tea or some trifle and doesn't ask for anything in return, we think of that person as tremendously kind. But such kindness pales in comparison with the generosity of our mother.

Our ability to speak, to conduct ourselves in society, and to get along with people are all gifts from our parents. Rather than be satisfied with our own cleverness, we should remember that there was a time when we didn't know how to say a single word, how to wipe, feed, clothe, or clean ourselves. Our mothers and fathers helped us learn to speak, walk, eat, and dress. They were our first teachers.

In this and countless previous lifetimes, beings have shown us kindness in all these worldly ways. They have also been essential to our spiritual development in that their liberation is the purpose of our practice, the foundation of our altruistic motivation, without which we could not attain enlightenment. Considering such things, we begin to experience profound gratitude and an awareness of the debt we owe.

So in cultivating equanimity, we acknowledge that all beings have been our mother at some time. Then we develop an appreciation for the kindness they have shown us and a wish to repay them. In this way we give rise to a higher motivation, that of benefiting all beings, not only on a temporary basis but with the most perfect form of repayment possible: attaining enlightenment so that we might help them do the same.

A Western student once told a lama, "I have a problem with thinking of beings as once having been my mother. My mother was never good to me. We had a bad relationship. So every time I meditate on bodhicitta, I think of my mother and get upset and angry. Can I just forget thinking about my mother for now?"

The lama answered that the idea is to develop compassion for everybody, including one's mother, but that the order in which one does it doesn't matter. He said that in Tibet and India people regard the mother as the kindest, most wonderful person imaginable. When a beginner needs an easy entrance into practice, the teacher uses those feelings for the mother as a basis for developing warmth and compassion for others.

The lama added, "If you find it easier to develop compassion for all other beings first, and then for your mother, that's all right. The point is ultimately to have compassion for everybody, including your mother."

Finally, we recognize the equality of all beings in that the intrinsic nature of each one, from the smallest insect to the greatest realization holder, is primordial purity. Having come to understand this equality—in that all want to be happy, all suffer, all have shown us the kindness of parents, and all have buddha nature—we arouse compassion for all of them by recognizing their tragedy: although they want only to be happy, out of ignorance they create conditions that perpetuate their suffering.

Compassion itself, the aspiration that suffering cease, is the second immeasurable quality. A powerful antidote to self-centeredness, compassion releases us in the short term from relentlessly focusing on ourselves and our problems. It is beneficial in the long term because even one or two moments of heartfelt compassion purify enormous amounts of karma.

How do we generate compassion? We begin by contemplating the difficulties of others, then putting ourselves in their shoes. We start with the suffering in the human realm, because it might be difficult at first to contemplate the anguish of beings in other realms. We contemplate the distress of one or two people we know and slowly, with practice, expand our focus to include more and more, until everyone's suffering has true meaning for us. We imagine their pain so vividly that we can practically see it before our eyes.

Imagine someone close to you dying, perhaps in a hospital surrounded by family and friends. When her suffering seems palpable to you, put yourself in her place. Your cherished family and friends are crying, pleading with you not to die. The doctor has told you that you have only a few minutes to live. Breathing is becoming difficult and you're terrified, not knowing what awaits you. Everything familiar, even your own body, will be left behind.

Not a penny of the money you've accumulated will go with you; not a single friend or family member will follow, no matter how dear they might be.

Or instead of contemplating the misery of a person you know, you might imagine someone living in a drought-ridden country where families, even entire villages, are dying of starvation. Put yourself in that person's place. Picture yourself among the few beloved family members who haven't already died, who are lingering on the brink of death. You know that you too will soon die; there is nothing left to eat. You and your relatives are too weak to help each other. You are all powerless in the face of death.

You might imagine someone dying in war and then put yourself in that person's place. Your best friend has been killed and is lying next to you; you are wounded, bleeding to death, and can't move. Everyone around you is dying or too busy to notice you. You feel completely alone and terrified.

Or you might contemplate the plight of an elderly person. Envision a time when your own children, whom you've conscientiously raised for so many years, won't help or even listen to you. Perhaps they're looking forward to your death. You can no longer tend to yourself, and your children are too busy to care for you. Perhaps you're alone in a nursing home where your children visit only once or twice a year. Your friends don't respect you any longer; they won't listen to you anymore. You would like to get around and talk as you did when you were younger, but you lack the ability to do so.

As you examine each of these situations, tremendous fear will arise. At that point, ask yourself, "If I feel this much fear simply from contemplating such suffering, how must those who actually experience it feel?"

Then think about the many people throughout the world who are hurting others. They are creating negative karma that will eventually ripen and bring them harm, and they don't even realize it. They think they are doing the right thing but are only making matters worse.

As you contemplate in this way, compassion and the aspiration to help both those currently suffering and those planting seeds of future suffering will arise strongly in your heart. Acknowledge your own relative good fortune and then make the commitment to do everything you can to create benefit. You have heard the teachings of the dharma; you have learned some methods for purifying the causes of suffering. But these beings, all of whom have shown you the kindness of a mother, have nothing. How tragic.

In Mahayana Buddhism, great and equal compassion for all beings—whether friends or enemies—is essential. With this strong foundation, enlightenment will lie in the palm of your hand, even if you don't try to attain it. If, however, you don't develop compassion but are motivated only by the selfish desire to escape suffering yourself, you will not achieve the ultimate goal.

Compassion is enhanced by the third immeasurable quality: a love that reaches equally to all. Love is the sincere desire that each being experience both the cause and fruit of temporary and ultimate happiness. We establish a commitment to make every effort—physical, verbal, and mental—to bring this about.

When we strive toward the happiness of others, we must do so with pure heart. If there is some self-interest in our efforts, failure will cause us regret, which will nullify the virtue of our actions.

A method called *tonglen* can help us develop pure and selfless love for all beings. We begin by arousing compassion as we contemplate the painful condition of others. Then, as we inhale, we imagine breathing in the suffering and negative karma of all beings throughout every realm of experience in the form of black light. As we exhale, we visualize all of our love, happiness, and good fortune radiating out to them as white light.

At first you might feel reluctant to practice this meditation, fearing that it will harm you in some way. But if you have the selfless intention to help others, your doubts will vanish and the practice will increase your positive qualities. Only your fear itself can harm you, for it acts as a magnet that attracts negativity.

After practicing this meditation strongly with a pure heart, you will begin to see yourself as a vehicle for others' happiness. Not only will your love and compassion increase, but you will find yourself having fewer negative thoughts and committing fewer harmful actions. Your self-clinging will begin to loosen, and gradually your karma will be purified. Ideally, we develop the loving capacity of bodhicitta intention to such an extent that we would fearlessly, without hesitation or regret, give or do anything necessary to be of benefit.

In many of his lifetimes on the bodhisattva path, the being who became the Buddha Shakyamuni gave up his body for the sake of others. In one lifetime, he was the middle of three sons of a king. While lost in the forest with his two brothers, he came upon a starving tigress and her five cubs. The tigress could no longer move and had no milk to feed her litter. The prince thought, "How many times in my past lives have I tried to save myself? I've thought only of my own safety, and died again and again without benefiting anyone. My body is impermanent; it won't last long anyway. If it can be of use to this tigress and her cubs, so be it."

He sent his brothers off to search for food and lay down next to the tigress. She was too weak, however, to feed on him. Having no knife, the prince broke off a piece of bamboo, slit his wrist with it, and let the blood drip into her mouth. Then he cut off pieces of his flesh and fed them to her. As the tigress slowly gained strength, he lost more and more of his own. But he had no regret. He dedicated his life not only to the mother and her cubs, but to all other beings, and then he died.

At that moment, the boy's mother had a dream of three suns in the sky, the middle sun eclipsed. She awoke knowing that something had happened to her middle son and witnessed extraordinary phenomena—the earth shook, flowers rained down, music and songs of praise resounded.

The prince's hair and bones were placed in a *stupa,* a monument to the true nature of mind, at a sacred site known as Namo Buddha in Nepal. Many people still derive great benefit, purifying vast amounts of karma, by circumambulating that stupa.

The last of the four immeasurable qualities is rejoicing: delighting in other people's happiness. We rejoice in their worldly blessings—their health, wealth, wonderful relationships—and in their spiritual good fortune. We don't allow jealousy to overtake us and wonder, "Why don't I have what they have?" Instead, we make the wish that their happiness will be long-lived, and we do everything we can to make that happen.

By rejoicing in others' virtue and the happiness it creates, we accumulate as much merit as they do. Similarly, if we rejoice in others' nonvirtue or the suffering it creates, we make as much nonvirtue as they do.

During the time of the Buddha Shakyamuni, two boys were begging for food outside a king's palace. The king had invited the

Buddha and his retinue for a meal, and a very wonderful feast had been prepared. One boy began to beg for food before the Buddha was offered any. Nobody gave him anything to eat and he became very angry. He thought, "If I were a king, I'd chop off the head of the Buddha, and of this king, and of everyone who is helping him."

The other boy waited until the Buddha and his retinue had been served. Then he begged for leftovers and was given as much as he could eat. He thought to himself, "What a wonderful king. What great merit he has created by offering the Buddha a meal and by his generosity to those of us who are poor. If I were a king I would offer whatever I had to the Buddha, as well as to the poor."

When he had had his fill, the good-hearted boy wandered across the border into a nearby kingdom. He lay down to sleep, sheltered from the hot sun by the shade of a tree. Unbeknownst to him, the king of this region had died and his ministers were searching for someone with the qualities and merit to be the new king. The people in the village where the boy slept noticed that throughout the day, although the sun's position in the sky changed, the shade protecting the boy never shifted. Thinking this extraordinary, they reported it to the ministers.

When the ministers received this news, they ordered that the good-hearted boy be included among the candidates for the throne, who were to appear at a large gathering of all the king's subjects. The new king would be chosen by a very special elephant. On the appointed day, the elephant approached the poor, bedraggled boy—who stood at the very back of the group of candidates—anointed his head with consecrated water from a vase, lifted him up with his trunk, and placed him on the throne.

Meanwhile, the angry boy slept in the king's garden. A passing chariot lost control and careened over his body, crushing his neck and killing him.

Practicing the four immeasurable qualities requires effort at first. One by one, we release the knots that bind us—mind's poisons and delusions. Equanimity reduces pride, rejoicing reduces jealousy, compassion reduces desire, and love reduces anger and aversion. As anger wanes, mirror-like wisdom dawns; as desire wanes, discriminating wisdom dawns; and so forth. As our practice matures and wisdom is revealed, the four immeasurable qualities arise naturally, effortlessly, just as rays of light and warmth radiate from the sun.

Although many think they can recognize wisdom directly, it's not so easy. Until the knots begin to release, awareness will not be evident. It is through the four doors of love, compassion, joy, and equanimity that we can enter the mandala of the absolute nature of mind.

QUESTION: We may superficially accept that the motivation for practicing is to benefit others, yet in truth want to keep some of the benefit for ourselves to solve our own problems. What is your advice?

RESPONSE: We need to understand the limitations of a self-centered approach, to realize that our deeply ingrained self-focus will ultimately prevent us from attaining liberation and omniscience, both of which we need to benefit others. With this understanding, we can begin to develop an altruistic motivation. It takes time, patience, and diligence, but if we meditate on bodhicitta again and again, our motivation will gradually change. Most of us start out with very little altruism. The more we practice and contemplate the shortcomings of selfish motivation and the benefits of selfless motivation, the more the scales will tip, until our self-concern is equal to our concern for others. As our altruism becomes predominant, we will finally get to a point where there is no self-cherishing, where we care only for the welfare of others.

15

Wishing and Engaging Bodhicitta

BODHICITTA HAS TWO frameworks: the welfare of others, or compassion; and enlightenment, or wisdom. We wish for enlightenment not just to escape samsara but also to benefit whoever sees, hears, touches, or remembers us. Right now we might have the ability to help ten, a hundred, a thousand, or, if we are famous, perhaps millions of people. But that isn't enough. Limitless beings suffer throughout samsara.

When we practice, we can give rise to one of three forms of bodhicitta. We call the first the *shepherd-like attitude,* in that our motivation is to follow those we're guiding to enlightenment just as a shepherd herds his sheep through the gate, then follows after. The second is called the *ferryman's* or *boatman's attitude.* In crossing a river, the boatman arrives at the opposite shore at the same time as his passengers. In the same way, we reach enlightenment together. Realistically, however, in order to free others from the cycles of existence, we must first free ourselves. Just as a king assumes the throne first and then rules the kingdom wisely, in our practice we aspire to attain buddhahood ourselves so that we can free others from samsara. This is known as the *kingly attitude.* We cultivate one or the other of these forms of bodhicitta to counteract various degrees of self-clinging, the greatest single impediment to enlightenment.

Aspiring to attain enlightenment for ourselves and all beings is called *wishing bodhicitta*. Although essential to our practice, it alone will not accomplish our goal. Wishing bodhicitta is like looking at the vast ocean of samsara and wanting to get ourselves and others to the opposite shore. If we don't have a boat and a means to propel it, no amount of wishing will get us across.

We must also become actively involved—we have to actually enter the path of practice. Fully utilizing the methods that reduce and purify negative thoughts and actions and enhance positive qualities, while simultaneously recognizing the true nature of mind so that we can liberate ourselves and others is called *engaging bodhicitta*. This is the way of the bodhisattva.

One method of incorporating bodhicitta into every aspect of our lives is to practice the *six perfections* (in Sanskrit, *paramitas*): generosity, moral discipline, patience, diligence, concentration, and wisdom.

Generosity loosens our grip on the things we cling to. There is the material generosity of sharing food, clothing, and other things of substance; the spiritual generosity of imparting spiritual teachings, of providing freedom from fear and protection to those who are afraid; and the generosity of effort, giving freely of our time and energy as well as our words in sharing, teaching, counseling, and expressing loving kindness to benefit others. Whatever fortune we presently enjoy is the fruit of our past generosity, which we can now rejoice in sharing.

In the practice of moral discipline, we continually check our motivation to ensure that we use our body, speech, and mind skillfully, that we are not only truly harmless but helpful. In addition, we strive to create conditions that will enable us to produce the greatest benefit—learning what we need to learn, pulling together the necessary resources, and so on. Finally, we remain tireless in our discipline.

There are three kinds of patience: forbearance in the face of threats or harm from others, accepting the hardships of spiritual practice, and relating without fear to the profound implication of the true nature of reality.

We practice patience by relentlessly pursuing our efforts to benefit others no matter what their reaction or attitude toward us. We also develop patience as an antidote to aggression, anger, and hatred. A Buddhist proverb says, "For an evil such as anger, there is no practice like patience." It contributes to our peace of mind and ultimately to the attainment of enlightenment.

Whenever an individual or a group creates problems for others, instead of reacting to their aggression with anger, we remind ourselves that all beings have been our mothers and shown us great kindness, that out of ignorance they neither understand this connection nor realize that they are planting seeds of suffering. By not responding in kind we benefit all those involved, because our forbearance very quickly diffuses aggression, thus minimizing further problems.

As the Buddha Shakyamuni sat under the bodhi tree in Bodh Gaya, India, the forces of Mara—the embodiment of all that binds us to samsara—called together a great host of demons in a last attempt to defeat and prevent the Buddha from attaining enlightenment. Though they attacked him, the power of the patience, love, and compassion that arose naturally from his realization turned their weapons into flowers.

Diligence involves preparing for and beginning a task, donning armor-like perseverance to see it through, and, finally, never turning back. We develop not only our positive qualities, but also

the means to benefit others. Someone may have abundant loving kindness and the intention to help heal the sick, but he must
first spend years studying and training. We practice diligence
to achieve our goal: the temporary and ultimate happiness of
all beings. If it's difficult to move one step forward, at least we
shouldn't back up. Slowly, step by step, even a donkey can make
its way around the world.

We develop concentration, or meditative stability, by training
the mind. The Tibetan term for this perfection is *samten, sam*
meaning "to think," to use the rational mind in contemplation, and *ten* meaning "stable" or "firm." The mind comes to
rest one-pointedly, either upon an idea or in the natural state of
awareness.

One type of meditative stability involves thinking about or
focusing on a single idea without distraction so that the mind
doesn't wander to other—even parallel—ideas. Concepts and the
words that convey them point us to a deeper meaning. Another
kind involves letting the mind fall naturally into its fundamental
state, unobscured by thoughts of the three times—past, present,
and future. Yet another, more profound form of meditative stability is imbued with the sixth perfection of wisdom, which acts
as a seal applied to the state of calm abiding.

Wisdom, also called transcendent knowledge, means knowledge of absolute truth beyond ordinary concepts, subject–object
duality, and temporary experiences of bliss, clarity, and stability.
Beyond this, there is nothing to be known. Beyond this, there is
no goal.

The first five of the six perfections function within a dualistic
framework. In the case of generosity, we speak of the subject, oneself, who gives; the object, the person to whom something is given;

and the act of giving. The subject, object, and the action between them are called the *three spheres*.

Belief in the solidity of the three spheres is the domain of relative truth. Reality has two aspects: ultimate reality, or absolute truth—things as they are in and of themselves—and relative reality, or relative truth—things as they appear to be on a conventional level. The Tibetan term for relative truth consists of *kun*, meaning "all" or "many," and *dzob*, "that which is not true." So *kundzob* implies the display of myriad phenomena that appear to be something they are not.

Like children chasing after a rainbow, we treat the dreamlike display of appearances as substantial and real. Yet nothing about those appearances is permanent. A mountain is not permanent; it can be washed away, bulldozed, or blown apart. It is not singular; it is composed of dirt, rocks, and gravel. Nor is it free; things affect it all the time. Similarly, our body is not permanent; it changes constantly, and some day it will no longer exist. It is not singular, but a composite of bones, nerves, muscles, blood, and flesh. Nor is it free; external influences can affect it. Examining thoughts in the same way, we find they are not permanent, singular, or free. In fact, this holds true of everything in our ordinary reality.

Phenomenal appearances are illusory. Lost in the labyrinth of our experiences by habit and training, most of us believe them to be true just as we believe the events in a dream to be true. In our all-consuming involvement with ordinary reality, we invest things with a truth and permanence they don't have. As we do, circumstances become more complex, and suffering deeper. We're caught in samsara like flies on flypaper, unable to discover our true nature, the source of fulfillment.

We consider phenomenal appearances to be true because, in the context of our dreamlike experience, so they seem. Fire, while not permanent, singular, or free, can burn our flesh. In this sense, our relative experience is true. At the same time, the ultimate nature of experience remains unchanging and absolutely pure—empty, just as the night dream experience is empty. In the night dream, things appear to take place, yet upon awakening we realize that nothing really occurred. This is the true nature of all samsara.

When we overcome our assumption that phenomena are permanent, singular, and free of outer influences, our delusion erodes, and the essence of experience—pure awareness—shines through. The veneer of false assumption becomes progressively thinner until it cracks, and we directly encounter our true nature.

The great Shantideva of Buddhist India said that absolute truth is not the province of the ordinary mind, which is concerned with conventional reality. Ultimate reality remains free of and beyond all conceptual elaborations—one cannot say that things exist, nor that they do not exist, that they are or are not. As we listen to teachings, contemplate, and meditate, our intellectual understanding gradually develops into deeper knowing, direct experience, and finally the stable realization of our absolute nature. Then we discover that, as a famous Tibetan prayer states, the absolute truth is not some *thing* that exists, for even the Buddha cannot see it. Nor can we assert that relative reality does not exist at all, for how then would we account for all samsara and nirvana—the unceasing display of phenomenal appearances? There is no contradiction in saying that the fundamental nature of things is unchanging, though on the relative level it manifests as a constantly changing, ephemeral display; that just as in a dream, phenomena do not ultimately exist, although they manifest. Because of this we say that phenomena are *empty*.

The empty nature of our experience—the birthless, deathless nature in which nothing has ever come or gone, the nature beyond the extremes of existence and nonexistence—is inseparable from the unceasing display of manifest appearances. The actual nature of our relative experience is the absolute truth. The knowledge that absolute and relative truth are inseparable is called *view*.

When we apply view to our practice of the first five perfections, we go beyond their ordinary meaning. If in a dream we give an apple to a beggar, in truth there is no apple, no beggar. When our generosity is imbued with wisdom—recognition of the true nature of the three spheres—it becomes the perfection of generosity. Knowing that our actions undertaken to benefit others are empty of inherent existence, yet acting nonetheless, is the essence of the practice of the six perfections and of the path of the bodhisattva.

The act of benefiting and the effortful gathering of virtue result in the *accumulation of merit*. To create benefit within the relative dream experience, we harness the mind's duality using skillful methods such as the first five perfections in a conceptual framework. Effortless practice—maintaining awareness within a nonconceptual framework—results in the *accumulation of wisdom*. Here "awareness" refers to the nonconceptual recognition of the true nature of the three spheres. We don't fall to the extreme of affirming that everything exists as it appears, nor do we go to the other extreme of denying that anything is happening.

Because the ground of our experience consists of both relative and absolute truth, the accumulation of both merit and wisdom is essential to our practice; both are indispensable for attaining enlightenment. The path of the bodhisattva is the union, or inseparability, of these two accumulations. We practice maintaining view in the midst of our daily lives, acting skillfully on a conventional level without ever losing awareness of the essential nature of our activity. This awareness is the ultimate aspect of bodhicitta, while the compassionate aspiration to benefit beings is the relative.

Practice of the two accumulations leads to the realization of the two kayas: the formless aspect of enlightened mind, dharmakaya; and the expression of that ultimate realization for the benefit of others, the form kaya, or rupakaya. Thus the ground of our experience is the union of the two truths, and our path the union of the two accumulations, which leads to the fruition: the union of the two kayas, the form and formless aspects of enlightened being.

The merit we create through our practice can be dedicated to the benefit of all beings. If we were in a dark house, the light from one butterlamp could illuminate an entire room and everyone present would benefit. When all the oil was burned, the light would go out. Whoever added oil to the lamp would make the light last longer, and everyone would benefit. In a similar way, whoever creates virtue and dedicates it to all beings helps the collective merit of all beings last longer.

Shantideva said that just as a mountain of dry grass the size of Mount Meru can be reduced to ashes by a single spark, merit gathered over eons that has not been dedicated can be destroyed by a single instant of anger. If we practice virtue with bodhicitta motivation and dedicate the resulting merit to the benefit of all beings, it can't be destroyed. To enhance the power of our dedication, we can pray that it will be the same as that of all buddhas and bodhisattvas, who have always dedicated their virtue to the benefit of others and always will.

To turn the mind toward selflessness, we need to contemplate bodhicitta again and again, just as we do the four thoughts. Imagine yourself experiencing someone else's suffering, then let the mind rest. Reestablish your commitment to do everything you can to relieve the suffering of beings and to help them find liberation, to awaken from the dream of suffering. Pray that, by the blessings of all sources of refuge, your aspirations will be fulfilled. Then give rise to unbiased compassion for the suffering of all beings—those who suffer in the moment and those who will suffer when their negative karma ripens. Contemplate the kindness they have all shown you, the kindness of a mother. Then allow the mind to rest, arouse compassion, reestablish your commitment, pray, and so on.

If you do this throughout the day, turning for brief periods of time to each of these stages of meditation, your mind will change. Samsaric experience is like being trapped in a bag. Each time you bring the mind back to meditation, you poke a small hole in the bag. If you do this many times, it will start to shred until finally you can break free. When we bring pure motivation to everything we do, all of our activities become part of our practice.

QUESTION: In order for our compassion to have an effect, shouldn't we go out into the world and do something like help the homeless?

RESPONSE: It's good to want to help in a specific way but you must be careful, because the poisons of the mind can stain your actions. You might think, "If I help the homeless, then I'm a good person." Or you might feel, "I'm a little better than the homeless because I'm providing for them." Or you might say, "I'd better help the homeless so that no one thinks I'd let people sleep on the street." If a man insults you when you give him a piece of bread and you get angry, or if he smiles at you and you're happy, your action is stained by pride, attachment, or aversion. These poisons can function in a very subtle manner. This is a place where many people get stuck.

Maybe you can help a thousand people, maybe even ten thousand. But they might hate you for it, or your efforts may not do much good and they'll be left as miserable as ever, no freer sleeping on a cot than on the sidewalk.

This doesn't mean we should be apathetic. We must do everything we can to relieve others' suffering in the moment. But at the same time we need to expand the scope of our motivation, addressing the ultimate needs of all beings. It's important not to get shortsighted and focus on the human condition to the exclusion of other realms. The suffering of the homeless, while terrible, is not as great as that of beings in the hell realms. Immediate needs are different from ultimate needs. We can't be naive about this.

Before we can be truly effective in helping others, we need to develop our positive qualities. Then we won't respond to anger with anger, but with compassion. We need to know how to swim in order to save someone who is drowning. Otherwise, though we mean to help, we'll only drown as well.

In short, we have to practice meditation, because it will give us the ability to do much more for others. Eventually, we can help them on both an immediate and an ultimate level. We can't think, "I don't have time to meditate because I have to work in the soup kitchen." We have to do both simultaneously.

If we experience personally what it is to suffer, we can understand what suffering is like for others. Otherwise, working for the sake of others becomes theoretical. If your child fell into a deep hole, you would do anything you could to get him out. Your heart would break until you could lift him to safety. You should feel the same about all other beings, who have been both your own children and your parents.

But compassion isn't enough. If you think that you can help homeless people simply by taking them off the sidewalk and giving them food and shelter, your understanding is limited. Instead, you need to determine the root of the problem and find a way to bring not only temporary but ultimate benefit. Otherwise, you may spend your whole life trying to help people and not get anywhere. You won't find liberation, nor will the people you have tried to help. You might attempt to make a better "dream" for yourself or others. But depending on what's at play in your mind as you act, you might not be able to accomplish even that much.

If, however, you have a pure heart with motivation that is selfless, all-encompassing, and unstained by the poisons of the mind, then even the most insignificant-seeming action can produce great merit, much more so than actions that are only outwardly virtuous.

Motivation determines the degree of virtue or nonvirtue produced by each action. When you offer something, the merit you gather doesn't have as much to do with the object you are offering as with your motivation. If you offer your most valued possession for selfish reasons, the benefit is very small. But if you offer something very small with pure motivation, the resulting merit is enormous.

There was once a great meditator in retreat who practiced

diligently day and night. One day, knowing that the sponsor of his retreat was coming to visit, he carefully cleaned his shrine, water bowls, and meditation room. As he sat back down, he asked himself, "Why did I do that? My motivation wasn't pure." So he got back up and threw ashes on the shrine and throughout the room.

Honesty is certainly a virtue and it's important to speak the truth, but you should do so with the proper motivation. Are you speaking the truth because you feel you're right or because you see that doing so will benefit the situation? If you're only trying to prove your point, you're simply acting out of pride.

Suppose a desperate-looking man runs past you and ducks into a doorway. A few minutes later a person with a knife comes running by and asks, "Where did he go?" Are you going to give him away, or are you going to claim that you have never seen the person? In this situation, a bodhisattva would choose to lie, fully prepared to suffer the consequences, for she wouldn't want the man to be killed or the murderer to create the negative karma of killing.

What may seem a nonvirtuous act can actually be virtuous if it is performed for the right reason. It might seem nonvirtuous or shameful to hit your child. But if spanking him is the only way to keep him from harming himself or someone else, then it is actually of great benefit.

QUESTION: If we are always thinking about others, how do we take care of ourselves?

RESPONSE: The best way to take care of ourselves is to take care of others. The merit created by this selfless approach to life becomes the cause of our own happiness.

There was a man living at the time of the Buddha who was plagued by problems with his relationships, family, and finances. Things got so bad that he decided to find the Buddha and ask him what to do.

On his journey he met a snake, who asked him where he was going. The man told him he was going to the Buddha to seek help. The snake replied, "I need help, too. At night it's very easy for me to come outside of my hole, but in the daytime it's very difficult to get back in. Could you please ask the Buddha what the problem is?" The man agreed to do so and continued on his way.

After a while he came upon a bird singing in a tree. The bird asked where he was going and the man replied as before. The bird said, "Could you ask a question for me, too? When I sit in this tree, my song is very beautiful. But when I sit in other trees, it isn't the same. I'm curious to know why. Could you ask the Buddha?" The man agreed to do so and continued on. He felt a strong commitment to the two animals and kept their questions in his heart.

Finally, the man found the Buddha and asked the animals' questions. The Buddha replied, "At night nothing annoys the snake, but in the daytime many insects bother him, which makes him angry. When he's angry, his body puffs up and it becomes difficult for him to get back into his hole. Tell him to practice patience and he won't have a problem. As for the bird, a golden vase filled with jewels, hidden below the tree, is what makes her song so lovely."

With gratitude the man set out for home. On his way, he told the bird and the snake what the Buddha had said, but when he got home, he realized that he hadn't asked his own questions. He'd kept the two animals so firmly in his mind that he had completely forgotten his own problems.

Then it occurred to him that, like the snake, he had a problem with anger. He needed to practice patience, just as the Buddha had instructed the snake to do. He also realized that if he asked the bird for even one of the jewels buried under the tree, he could solve all his financial problems. By focusing on and serving the needs of others rather than his own, he also benefited.

If we want to bring about happiness, we should always focus on others' needs. If we would rather cause suffering, we should think only of ourselves.

QUESTION: Sometimes I try so hard to do my best, but don't feel that my actions have much impact.

RESPONSE: There is a story about a woman who went to a beautiful temple in Lhasa to pay her respects to a sacred statue of the Buddha, said to have been blessed by the Buddha himself. Being very poor, the woman had nothing more to offer than a cup of turnip soup. She said to the Buddha statue, "Well, you may not like turnip soup, but this is all I've got and this is what I'm offering." It's a bit like that for us. We may feel that what we have to offer is inadequate, but if we do the best we can, that's all we can do.

Again, what it comes down to is motivation. There was once a man who generated great virtue by creating *tsa-tsas,* small molded sculptures symbolizing enlightened mind. One day the man carefully placed one of these sculptures by the side of the road and left.

Another man came along, saw that rain was hitting the tsa-tsa, and thought, "How sad. It's going to get ruined." The only thing he could find for protection was the discarded sole of a shoe. So he placed this over the sculpture and left.

A third man came along, saw the sole on top of the tsa-tsa, and thought, "This is horrible. Someone has disrespectfully put the sole of a shoe on top of this image of enlightened mind." So he threw the sole away.

Each man had equally virtuous intentions, and the actions of each contributed toward his eventual realization of enlightened mind.

QUESTION: Can the same action under different circumstances produce different amounts of merit?

RESPONSE: It depends partly on your motivation and partly on the recipient of your offering. Being generous to a starving, destitute, or desperate person produces greater merit than extending generosity to someone more fortunate, because the gratitude and rejoicing of a needy person are so much greater. There is more merit in making an offering to a spiritual practitioner than to a nonpractitioner, because the practitioner dedicates the merit generated by the act. The same offering given to a practitioner with greater realization will produce even more merit, because of the power of realization that she brings to her dedication of merit to those with whom she has a connection, as well as to all beings.

The difference between having pure motivation and not is like the difference between walking and taking a jet. Virtuous acts and spiritual practice based on bodhicitta create millions of times more virtue than acts that are not so motivated. They create the greatest benefit and ensure enlightenment. This is true in daily life as well as in our formal practice. We mustn't rush through liturgies, mindlessly chanting the refuge and bodhisattva vows, thinking we need to get on to the main practice.

Having a good heart remains the key. As much as you learn, as much as you practice, if you don't have a good heart you won't go very far. The benefit will only be temporary.

QUESTION: Could you say something about connecting with our true nature?

RESPONSE: It doesn't help much to talk about it. It's better just to drop our hope and fear, let the mind rest, and allow the experience of that which is beyond concepts to arise. It's not a dull or sleepy state or like being in a coma.

The Buddha said that our true nature simply is; there are no words for it. If you have words to explain it, you're relying on concepts and you've lost it. The truth is so close, yet we don't recognize it.

Like the horse that never left the stable, our true nature is not somewhere else; it's just that our concepts and the mind's poisons prevent us from recognizing it. As these are purified, we can realize our nature directly, just as it is.

A person who has never tasted sugar might ask someone else what it's like. The reply will probably be, "It's very sweet." But what is "sweet"? There really is no way to explain it—you have to taste it for yourself. In the same way, the direct experience of our true nature can't be explained with words.

QUESTION: Is there one horse in the stable or many?

RESPONSE: I'll say many because it's closer to the truth. If there were only one horse and only one person had it, the implication would be that others didn't have it. Yet all beings have buddha nature. However, if one person gains complete realization of her true nature, this doesn't mean that everyone becomes enlightened. Similarly, one being might have a hellish existence, but not all beings do. So we can't really say there is just one.

But if we think there are many horses, we start seeing differences, such as big horses or small, horses so many hands high, and so on. Yet there is no way to measure our nature, for emptiness has no boundaries. In this sense you could say we're speaking of one horse.

But ultimately you can't say either that there is just one horse or that there are many. You asked a question on a relative level and I'm answering it on a relative level. But the truth is really beyond "one" and "many."

QUESTION: Will contemplating the meaning of emptiness lead the mind to an actual experience of emptiness?

RESPONSE: If concepts could bring the mind to an experience of emptiness, everyone would know emptiness, because everyone is constantly thinking. So in one way the answer is no. Yet the conceptual process of contemplating, resting, arousing compassion, making a commitment, and praying purifies obscurations and creates merit, and in that way brings us closer to a genuine realization of emptiness.

QUESTION: You've mentioned so many methods. How do we know which one to use and when?

RESPONSE: Our small-minded perspective creates walls around us. The walls in this room create a boundary that makes the sky outside seem different from the space inside. Yet basically there is no difference between them. Similarly, there is fundamentally no difference between the true nature of our body, speech, and mind and that of enlightened beings. That absolute nature is unborn, unceasing, like the sky.

So how do we dissolve such walls? First we look at the suffering of others, arouse compassion, and allow the mind to rest. Then we imagine exchanging our own fortune for others' misfortune. Then, again, we allow the mind to rest.

When we begin meditation practice, we tend to rely on contemplation as a method for changing the mind. Then we gradually incorporate into our practice an awareness of the illusory quality of our experience, which brings compassion for those who don't understand this. As our view and practice deepen, we start to recognize the true nature of all appearances. The many waves that arise are not different from, but are the display of, the ocean. Without the ocean, there would be no waves. This understanding leads to a shift in perspective. It's not our outer experience that changes so much as how we see it. It's like wearing glasses with a different prescription.

If we have a fever, we take specific medicine to lower it. If our worldly attachments prevent us from practicing diligently, we contemplate samsaric suffering and impermanence, recognizing the illusory quality of our worldly life. If our focus is on our own selfish needs and desires, we contemplate the suffering of others and arouse compassion. To address the mind's duality, we allow the mind to rest. So to whatever poison or problem arises in the mind, we apply an antidote through meditation.

This is why the Buddha Shakyamuni gave us so many methods for cutting through mind's delusion. Each of us needn't practice every one of them, but we will all find methods that work for us at each stage of our spiritual development. There may be hundreds or thousands of medicines in a pharmacy, but each person takes only what he needs. No one medicine cures all illnesses, nor will one medicine necessarily be effective through the full course of an illness. After a fever has abated, for example, one might need a new medicine to remove toxins from the system.

The important thing is to recognize that we are sick and to follow through with treatment, diligently and carefully. Then change will inevitably come.

PART IV

Introduction to Vajrayana

16

Revealing Our
Foundational Nature

THE 84,000 METHODS taught by the Buddha fall into three
main categories. The first, the Hinayana path, is based on the
understanding that samsara is permeated by suffering and difficulty, that whatever happiness can be found is impermanent. One
who follows this path makes the firm decision to practice in order
to find freedom beyond suffering. By applying the methods of the
Hinayana, the practitioner develops the ability to go beyond the
cycles of suffering to an experience of joyousness and bliss.

In addition to this same view of suffering, the Mahayana, the
second category, teaches that everything—suffering and happiness, misfortune and fortune, all of which arise as the play
of karma—is illusory, like a dream, a mirage, or a reflection of
the moon in water. Basic to this path are the view of the inseparability of relative and absolute truth and the aspiration to
help all beings find liberation. Recognizing the great kindness
shown us by all beings, who have at one time been our mothers,
we aspire to attain enlightenment in order to help them awaken
to their true nature. We don't just wish for this to happen, but
diligently apply the methods by which enlightenment can be
attained. Through the practice of the six perfections, we develop
the ability to go beyond samsara and nirvana, to find complete
liberation. This is the bodhisattva path.

The third category of Buddhist practice is called the Vajra-yana. That which is "vajra" has seven qualities: it cannot be cut by *maras,* obstacles to enlightenment, nor grasped or separated by concepts; it cannot be destroyed by concepts, which invest appearances with a truth they do not have; it is the pure truth in that there is nothing wrong within it; it has no substance that has been compiled and can break apart; it is not impermanent, and is therefore stable and unmovable; it is unstoppable in that it is all-pervasive; and it is unconquerable in that it is more profound than everything else and thus fearless.

These are the seven qualities of our own true nature, the true nature of our body, speech, and mind. To better understand this nature, we can begin by considering that each of us has a physical body in which we experience sky and earth, friends and enemies, happiness and sadness. When this body lies down at night to sleep, even though it doesn't move from the bed, an entirely different display of body, sky and earth, friends and enemies arises—a dream-body, dream-speech, and dream-mind. Upon waking the next day, we again have the daytime experience of body, speech, and mind that we hold to be true. When we die and the body is left behind and buried or cremated, we have another experience of body, speech, and mind in the intermediate state between the end of this life and the beginning of the next, one somewhat similar to a dream, but more frightening and difficult. Then, we take rebirth and experience yet again another body, speech, and mind. If we completely accomplish the spiritual path, upon enlightenment we realize wisdom (or vajra) body, wisdom speech, and wisdom mind.

Thus there is continuity to the principle of body, speech, and mind. But if we try to find it, thinking it to be some "thing," and attempt to determine its size or shape, no matter how intelligent we may be, no matter how advanced our technology, we won't find anything we can point to as the true nature of body, speech, and mind. Yet we can't deny our experience. This nature is beyond concepts, beyond the measure of ordinary mind; it is what we call emptiness. It cannot be destroyed, changed, or stopped— it exhibits the seven vajra qualities. "Yana," meaning "vehicle," refers to the methods by which we reveal this vajra nature.

Vajrayana practice encompasses both the Hinayana and Mahayana. On these paths of the sutras, or Buddhist scriptures, we pay careful attention to our outer actions—abandoning harmful ones and cultivating helpful ones—while taming the mind, developing and enhancing its inner qualities.

The practice of the four immeasurable qualities is very important in the Mahayana tradition. In the Vajrayana as well, elaborate mandalas depict four doors facing the four directions, symbolizing these four qualities; they are doorways by which we enter the truth, the absolute nature of mind. In the eastern direction stands the door of compassion, in the southern direction is the door of love, in the western direction that of joy, and in the northern direction equanimity. The mandala represents the display of mind's intrinsic purity. As our obscurations are removed, pure qualities of mind arise in the form of the mandala and the appearance of the pureland, the deity, and all pure experience.

Further, because of the many obstacles that make it difficult to maintain the purity of heart we aspire to, we contemplate the four thoughts—precious human birth, impermanence, karma, and suffering—which are foundational to all Buddhist practice.

On the Vajrayana path, resting in the view of the absolute nature beyond extremes, we practice virtue and refrain from committing harmful actions. Although our intrinsic nature is vajra body, speech, and mind, we don't experience that to be true. To resolve this ignorance, we listen to and contemplate the Vajrayana teachings and then practice both effortful and effortless meditation. Effortless meditation—simply allowing the mind to rest in its true nature—is difficult for many people at first. So we use effortful practice to purify the mind's obscurations and transform ignorance into knowing; then effortless meditation can arise spontaneously. Once we recognize our absolute nature, our practice becomes that of maintaining this awareness, understanding the inseparability of form and emptiness as wisdom body, the body of the deity; of sound and emptiness as wisdom speech, the speech of the deity; and thought and emptiness as wisdom mind, the mind of the deity. With this view and the methods of the Vajrayana, we can reveal our inherent purity in a relatively short time.

Another name for the Vajrayana is "secret mantra path." As unenlightened beings, we are not aware of our buddha nature—it is concealed from us—so we refer to it as "self-secret." Also, though extremely potent and effective, the Vajrayana path is a delicate process by its very nature and hence not widely taught. We maintain a certain degree of privacy, preserving the very personal quality of working with and receiving direct transmission from a Vajrayana teacher. That is why deeper and more detailed teachings require a personal commitment from anyone who seeks training in Vajrayana practice.

The term "mantra" in "secret mantra path" refers to something that swiftly provides protection and shelter. Through the skillful application of the Vajrayana methods, we protect ourselves from confusion and the negative karma it produces, and can thus attain enlightenment in a single lifetime.

In the Vajrayana tradition, we must initially receive empowerment to ripen the mind and create receptivity to the teachings and practice. Without empowerment, we are not authorized to listen to the teachings or to practice, for our efforts would be no more fruitful than crushing sand to make oil.

We receive the foundation empowerment from a lama who carries the practice lineage. It can't be given through words and substances alone, for just as only a king has the power necessary to name the next, only a lama who carries the lineage and has gained accomplishment in practice can empower another person. Through the power of meditation, mantra recitation, and the symbolic use of substances, we are empowered to undertake both development and completion stage practice and to recognize the wisdom body, speech, and mind of the deity, which is none other than our own absolute nature.

Once we have received this foundation empowerment from the lama, through daily practice we receive the path empowerment. With our practice, we continuously purify obscurations and enhance the pure qualities of mind in order to develop and uphold the view to which we were introduced in the foundation empowerment.

Simply receiving empowerment is not enough. The heart essence of empowerment is *samaya,* our commitment to uphold daily practice and the vows we have taken. If we break that commitment, we will encounter inauspicious circumstances in this life and great difficulties in future lives. But by keeping our samaya we will quickly find liberation.

The foundation of our being is mind's essence, buddha nature. All beings, large or small, have this essential purity. Like gold embedded in ore, the truth of our nature—though beginningless, endless purity—isn't obvious to us but can be revealed through practice, just as refining reveals the gold inherent within ore.

This essence, from beginningless time, is completely insubstantial, empty. Although we might try to find characteristics by which to define and understand emptiness, it can't be conceived of by ordinary concepts. It is thus without sign or character. We need nothing more than to maintain recognition of our essential nature for the fruition—the complete realization of the full qualities of this inherent purity—to be revealed. What we reveal is not beyond this nature, and in that sense it is beyond wishing. There is nothing outside, nothing elsewhere, to aspire to in order for this to happen, so it is beyond wishing or aspiration.

Because we don't recognize our essential nature—because we don't realize that although appearances arise unceasingly, nothing is really there—we invest with solidity and reality the seeming truth of self, other, and actions between self and others. This intellectual obscuration gives rise to attachment and aversion, followed by actions and reactions that create karma, solidify into habit, and perpetuate the cycles of suffering. This entire process needs to be purified.

In the first of three successive stages of teaching, referred to as the First Turning of the Wheel of Dharma, the Buddha taught the four noble truths: the truth of suffering, its origin, the path by which it is eradicated, and its cessation. In the Second Turning, he taught that the true nature of all phenomena is empty, without sign or character, beyond aspiration: the foundational nature is emptiness, the path is without sign, and the fruition is beyond aspiration. In the Third Turning, he spoke of the full, infallible, resplendent qualities of mind's nature, the appearance of the clear light of wisdom.

The Vajrayana tradition teaches the inseparability, from beginningless time, of the unborn, absolute nature of mind beyond words and the pure qualities of the clear light of wisdom. All-pervasive, noncomposite, unchangeable, and pure—this is our own mind's nature. In the Vajrayana, we are introduced to these vajra qualities.

All appearances arise as the display of the dynamic energy of our foundational nature. Experience can manifest in two ways. The reflection of the nonrecognition of our nature arises as the impure experience of the three realms of samsara. Although we may intellectually understand that our nature is pure, this is not our ordinary perception; we don't see, feel, or think about things in a pure way. When we start to apply ourselves to the spiritual path, question and probe, listen to teachings, repeatedly contemplate and meditate on those teachings, we begin to experience a mixture of pure and impure perceptions. Through spiritual practice, we can purify obscurations and accomplish the fruition. Our intrinsically pure nature becomes completely apparent as a pure embodiment of wisdom, the full revelation of our wisdom nature and the display of pure appearances.

Why isn't this our current experience? All ordinary appearances of the elements—earth, fire, water, wind, and space—are in essence pure. But just as someone with jaundice sees a snow mountain as yellow, due to our obscurations we don't see things purely. This impure perception has become a deeply entrenched habit. Through spiritual practice, our lack of recognition can be purified and then, just as one cured of jaundice can see a snow mountain as white, we, like all buddhas, will see the display of purity as it is—the immeasurable mandala of the deity. Everything has been this way from beginningless time. It is not something created, but is the radiance of the inherent qualities of our foundational nature.

This purity of our nature, unchanging throughout the three times—past, present, and future—is now obscured, like the sun by clouds. Due to the infallible cause and effect of karma and the reflections of the poisonous mind, endless appearances of environment and body arise.

Through visualization in the development stage of Vajrayana, we practice recognizing the pure nature and qualities of the environment as the pureland, and those of body, speech, and mind as the body, speech, and mind of the deity. This purifies the obscurations of mind that create the grosser reflections of our lack of recognition—the three realms and the three doors of body, speech, and mind—transforming the habit of perceiving in an ordinary way.

In the completion stage, we purify subtler obscurations. We dissolve the visualization into emptiness and rest effortlessly in awareness of mind's nature.

In the Vajrayana we recognize that all possible phenomenal appearances of samsara and nirvana from beginningless time are equal, without separation or distinction within their completely pure buddha nature, like night-dream appearances within the absolute truth of the dream. With this view we apply method and wisdom, development and completion stage practice, which, like healing medicines, purify the habit of holding to these temporary reflections of delusion as solid and reveal our intrinsic purity.

Through repeated application of these methods, we fully realize the fruition: like clouds swept away to reveal the unchanging sky, our obscurations resolve and beginningless purity is revealed. Our foundational nature is realized as the inseparability of the three kayas. The resplendent, full qualities of dharmakaya appear as the sambhogakaya to tenth-level bodhisattvas and as the nirmanakaya to ordinary beings, creating unceasing benefit.

Because our nature is beginningless purity—*dharmata*—we don't need to do anything to or take anything from it, enhance or reduce it, to make it manifest. Rather, using the methods that are the path, we simply reveal it as it is. Then our lack of understanding of this nature, our mind's ordinary habits and delusions, which are reflected in the impure samsaric experience we call reality, completely resolves into the absolute nature.

The approach of the Vajrayana path is not one of starting with something and then adding certain causes and conditions in order to arrive at something different. We use awareness of the foundational nature to reveal it as the fruition of the path. We simply remove the temporary obscurations that impede this complete realization. If we contemplate and meditate repeatedly upon this understanding, it will be easy to find accomplishment by relying on the Vajrayana.

The Vajrayana tradition includes outer, inner, and secret methods of practice. When we engage in outer deity practice, what really is the deity? In essence, the absolute truth of our own mind and of all experience is the absolute deity. The deity is not something we invent but the spontaneous display of the absolute truth, the manifestation not of something ordinary but of wisdom. This is the mandala of bodhicitta mind.

The nature of all beings and of all phenomena is dharmata. Within the absolute nature, there is no distinction or separation between self and other. It is all of one taste. All phenomena arise inseparably from and are contained within that nature. Nothing in our experience—neither the elements, phenomena, nor even a single molecule—is beyond the absolute nature, basic space. It is all-pervasive and true.

If we don't recognize this nature, we experience ourselves and all phenomena to be different from the deity. In that a night dream is by nature all-pervasive emptiness, there is really no separation between ourselves and the land, the sky, and the water. When we wake up, we see that all of the unceasing experiences that arose in the dream were only mind's display, empty yet appearing. If we don't recognize that we're dreaming, it all seems to be separate and true in and of itself.

From the perspective of ordinary mind, we perceive differences between our day and dream bodies, between ourselves and others, between someone who helps us and someone who is difficult. Yet on the level of absolute truth, no one ever comes or goes. It is all the display of mind. If we don't know the nature of our experience, if we don't know the absolute deity, then we experience ourselves as separate from the deity; this lack of recognition keeps us bound by karma and obscuration. If we realize our nature as the deity, all boundaries—like walls in space—dissolve and we realize vajra body. By knowing and maintaining recognition of our absolute nature, we are able to fully accomplish and reveal our nature as the deity.

With one's realization of dharmakaya, benefit is accomplished for oneself, while the unceasing capacity to benefit others arises as the form kaya. Beings are aided in immeasurable ways by the qualities of great knowing, loving kindness, and spiritual energy, and by the power of great wisdom and the prayers and aspirations accumulated on the path to enlightenment. This display for the benefit of beings arises as the appearance of both peaceful and wrathful deities with their retinues—for example, the peaceful form of Manjushri with the wrathful aspect of Yamantaka, or the peaceful form of Vajrasattva with the wrathful aspect of Vajrakumara. In this pure wisdom display of the absolute nature of mind arises body: the form and color of the deity; speech: the mantra of the deity; and great mind: the inseparability of emptiness and compassion. The deity is an infallible source of benefit, capable of leading beings from samsara to enlightenment.

Because we are bound by obscurations and don't realize our nature as that of the deity, we practice this recognition by visualizing the deity and reciting mantra, making offerings and prayers. In this way we receive the blessings of those who have attained the heart of enlightenment. This is outer deity practice.

In the category of inner deity practice, we visualize within our own body as the deity the subtle, pure central channel, in which moves the wisdom wind, or subtle energy, and which contains the even more subtle wisdom spheres called *bindus* (*tiglés* in Tibetan).

Although our experience of ordinary impure body, speech, and mind arises as the display of karmic wind, the mandala of the deity remains within the channels of our subtle body. By visualizing this mandala, working with the movement of the subtle energies, and reciting mantra, we reveal our own nature as the deity and absolute bodhicitta beyond extremes, unchanging great bliss that resides in the heart.

In secret deity practice, we recognize that all of samsara and nirvana has always been equal within basic space beyond extremes, that there is nothing that can be made better or worse, that our mind's pure nature has always been unborn, spontaneous wisdom. With this understanding we have no need to place our hopes in an outer deity, nor is it necessary to exert effort. Through the most profound Buddhist method, called Great Perfection, we effortlessly and spontaneously attain liberation simply by abiding in recognition of the absolute nature within which everything is contained and from which all phenomena arise inseparably, like the ocean and waves, or the sun and its rays.

Why are there so many different paths? First of all, the Buddha taught many methods. Also, different lamas have different kinds of experience and expertise; students have differing capabilities and so require different approaches. Some feel the strongest connection to outer deity practice, others to inner deity practice, and still others to the secret level of practice.

It might seem easy to recognize the absolute deity, our buddha nature, and abide in that recognition. But in fact, because we're so mired in hope and fear, attachment and aversion, it is actually very difficult. We have a multitude of concepts and habits, and when many experiences arise, we find it hard to maintain recognition of their absolute nature. Thus when we begin Vajrayana practice, we focus on creating and dissolving the visualization; then we work with the inner practices and yogas; and gradually we approach the effortless completion stage and Great Perfection practice.

The teachings of the Buddhadharma are like a garden bursting with flowers of many colors and shapes. It isn't necessary to choose only one method, nor to try to apply them all.

An angry person can work with his anger and negativity using the wrathful methods found in the vehicle of *maha yoga*. In this practice we visualize wrathful manifestations of wisdom crushing embodiments of negativity, radiating sparks, and brandishing weapons. Those destroyed aren't outer beings, but our own poisons, our real enemies and demons. Self-clinging is embodied in Rudra, a very powerful being and the "owner" of samsara who is suppressed by embodiments of wisdom. In wrathful imagery we see the play of an inner war: wisdom liberating anger, attachment, and ignorance.

Someone with very strong desire can use it as the path rather than abandoning it, working with the channels and energies of the subtle body, as well as the source of inner heat and bliss. Depictions of deities in union with their consorts do not represent ordinary desire or male–female relationships, but rather the inseparability of emptiness and great bliss. On the level of inner union, the subtle channels of the body are male and the subtle energies are female; inner heat is female and inner bliss, male. The union of these produces not ordinary but inexhaustible bliss. By working with desire, practitioners of *anu yoga* experience bliss, ultimately realizing the inseparability of great bliss and emptiness. Through this practice, they purify karma, accumulate merit, and reveal wisdom.

The paths of maha yoga and anu yoga involve effort, diligence, and consistency. For lazy practitioners whose predominant mental poison is ignorance, there is a third path, Great Perfection, or *ati yoga*. This path involves resting effortlessly in subtle recognition of the nature of mind. It is called the path of effortless effort. All the teachings and levels of practice up to the Great Perfection involve ordinary concepts, ordinary intelligence, and ordinary effort. But in Great Perfection, awareness itself is the path. Great Perfection practitioners use the method of the absolute deity, their own intrinsic awareness.

Each of these three approaches purifies obscurations. Which one we use depends on which poison predominates in our mind: that is the door to practice we stand closest to. Whichever is strongest and most familiar to us becomes the means by which we chip away at all the mind's obscurations.

Through the various methods of the Vajrayana path, we bring three elements to our practice: the purification of obscurations, ripening of the mindstream, and enhancement of the mind's positive qualities. By these means we are able to swiftly purify samsaric experience and realize the fruition beyond samsara and nirvana: the three kayas, our all-completing foundational nature. Wisdom is not born in us but rather becomes obvious, supporting and ripening our practice.

QUESTION: I find it very hard to accept a lot of what you are saying. Could you speak to my concern? I'm sure I am not the only one who feels this way.

RESPONSE: It's understandable if some of the teachings of the Vajrayana are difficult to accept at first. I never saw a watch until I was twenty-four years old. A friend of mine, another lama, purchased a brand new one from some crafty trader for an exorbitant sum. The trader said, "The special thing about this gadget is that whoever wears it will know exactly when he's going to die. You see these hands going around? They tell you exactly how much time you've got left." The lama had never seen a watch before, so he paid the price. Later he told me, "You know, it really seems to be true. See those little things going around? I guess they're slowly moving toward my death."

How could either of us have known? What reason did we have

to believe or disbelieve? I was a little skeptical, but I thought it might be true.

Later, when I first heard about the telephone, about people talking to one another across miles of mountains and rivers, I said, "That's impossible! Nobody can do that! You can shout long distances, but nobody can hear someone hundreds of miles away." I thought it was nonsense. Eventually, though, I encountered a telephone myself.

Then a friend told a group of us, "There is a little box you can look into and watch people dancing and talking and moving around. It's just like real life!" You should have seen our eyes! I was sure this was a lie. But there really are boxes in which you can see these things. You really can talk to people miles and miles away.

People have a habit of believing what is familiar to them and refusing to believe what is new. Many in the West doubt that there are past and future existences, simply because they have no personal knowledge of them. They don't remember having died and having been reborn, so they say reincarnation isn't possible. Their opinion is based upon ignorance, just as much as is someone's firm belief that a television couldn't exist.

The most productive way to listen to the teachings is to keep an open mind and suspend judgment. Spiritual practice removes increasingly subtle layers of obscuration. The more practice we do, the more we will realize directly, through our own experience, what is possible and true.

QUESTION: Are you saying that samsara is the pureland, and vice versa? Are they one and the same thing?

RESPONSE: Yes and no. You can say that ice is water; the essential nature of ice is not different from water. And yet ice has its own characteristics: as a solid, its appearance differs from that of water. Similarly, though samsara is not ultimately different from a pure realm of experience, it has its own characteristics. If we don't remove the mind's delusions, we see only those characteristics.

In general, we perceive phenomena in an ordinary way. We see things impurely—always zeroing in on the negative and focusing on what is wrong. This is simply our habit. Through Vajrayana practice, we recognize that the true nature of samsara is a pureland, pure experience. We're not pretending that something is what it's not. We just don't see it as it really is—and that is why we practice. By maintaining recognition of our true nature, we turn up the heat, take off the chill, and seemingly solid relative appearances resume their natural form, like ice melting. In essence, we are never other than the deity, and the environment is never other than a pureland, though we don't perceive this as long as we remain subject to the chill of mind's delusion.

If the true nature of samsara were fully obvious to us, we would be enlightened—we wouldn't need to practice. Only when our temporary obscurations are removed through practice is our foundational nature revealed.

QUESTION: Are there any tricks to maintaining pure view?

RESPONSE: It has always been our habit to see things in an ordinary way. And so in a sense, there are no tricks. We simply need to apply the methods of the Vajrayana diligently and consistently. If we could maintain clear recognition of our true nature, we would experience reality as a pureland. Even if we tried, we wouldn't find anything ordinary. Having accomplished some purification through our spiritual practice, we now have a "mixed" view. We enjoy clear perception in one moment, but in the next our obscurations create strong negativity. If we acknowledge our impure perception and understand the benefit of pure view, we will be motivated to practice in order to change our view.

There was once a woman whose merchant son promised to find her a relic of the Buddha's body during his travels. On his return from India, he realized he'd forgotten his promise. Coming upon a dog's tooth by the side of the road, he wrapped it in silk and gave it to his mother, telling her that it was one of the Buddha's teeth. With great devotion she placed it on her shrine, and day and night for the rest of her life, she prayed to the dog's tooth with deep faith, making prostrations, offerings, and praises. Over time, relics spontaneously arose from the tooth and rainbows appeared. Of course, this was due to the power of the Buddha's blessings and her faith and pure view, not to the dog's tooth!

QUESTION: How did we become so confused? Has our foundational nature always been obscured?

RESPONSE: The basic problem is lack of recognition of our true nature. All the teachings tell us this. Just as someone who is tightly bound with a rope can be freed by loosening the last knot to be tied, then the next to the last, and so forth, as you practice you will develop deeper insight, receive more profound teachings, such as those of the Great Perfection, and come closer to understanding the origin of the problem.

QUESTION: Why are mantras so powerful?

RESPONSE: The Sanskrit term *mantra* (*ngag* in Tibetan) connotes something praiseworthy, for repetition enables us to accomplish our goals easily and swiftly. The effectiveness of mantras is due to four factors. The first is their essential nature— the true nature of reality: they themselves do not deviate from emptiness, dharmakaya. The second is their inherent nature: on the phenomenal level of reality, they consist of sounds and syllables that arise spontaneously from the equanimity and compassion of buddhas, bodhisattvas, realization holders, and advanced spiritual practitioners. The third is the blessings that derive from the practice of realized beings who have consecrated them with their pure motivation, their prayers of aspiration, and their realization of the inseparability of deity and mantra. The fourth is the energy and power of mantras: those who recite them repeatedly and one-pointedly with faith purify karma and obscurations, receive blessings, and gain spiritual accomplishment.

QUESTION: What is the difference between the deities we rely upon in practice and the beings in the god realms?

RESPONSE: The same Tibetan word is used for both: *lha*. But the gods and goddesses of cyclic existence and the deities we meditate on are as different as gold and brass. Meditational deities are a reflection of mind's true nature, manifesting in different forms for the benefit of beings. Gods and goddesses are beings who, because of their positive karma and merit, take higher rebirth in the desire realm or in the form and formless realms— increasingly subtle and refined states of samsaric existence. Although positive karma can sustain some god realm beings for eons in a state of bliss—and it is possible that such gods may create some short-term benefit in other realms—at some point the momentum of positive karma ends and other predominant karmic patterns propel these beings into a lower rebirth.

QUESTION: When I visualize, I feel an energy. Is that just my imagination, or am I really feeling something?

RESPONSE: When we visualize, we blend our mind with the enlightened qualities of the deity, which helps to bring forth the same qualities inherent within us. In that way we receive the deity's blessings. You are feeling energy, in the sense that something is happening in your mind. That's one reason we do visualization practice.

QUESTION: It is difficult for me to visualize. I've never seen a deity; I can't relate to deities. Why can't I visualize a waterfall or garden as an example of purity—something I can see, something that represents part of my experience?

RESPONSE: There is a reason we rely on the deity. Deities are a manifestation of the pure qualities of enlightened mind, such as wisdom, compassion, and loving kindness. Visualizing an embodiment of such qualities has a much greater impact on the mind than visualizing something from our ordinary experience.

Visualization practice is effective because it is based on the truth, not on pretense. It's not as though we're donkeys pretending to be horses. Our true nature and that of all beings remains the boundless purity embodied in the deity.

The absolute nature of all the elements is emptiness, yet on the relative level their qualities are not the same. The nature of both fire and water is emptiness. But we can't burn something with water, and we can't wash something with fire. A vast array of distinct qualities and capacities arises from emptiness. In essence, a waterfall and a deity are the same, but on the relative level the benefit that arises from visualizing them is very different.

QUESTION: Through visualization practice, will we actually see the deity?

RESPONSE: The three doors of body, speech, and mind are inherently the three vajras: vajra body, speech, and mind—the body, speech, and mind of the deity. Development stage practice, in which we visualize our body, speech, and mind as those of the deity, purifies the ordinary mind's habit of conceiving of appearances as solid and real. Through the refining away of impurities that create the perception of difference between ourselves and the deity, the fictitious boundary slowly dissolves. Then the indwelling mandala of the deity that is the pure display of the true nature of reality can become apparent.

QUESTION: Will practitioners experience different results or types of realization depending on which deity they focus on in their practice?

RESPONSE: Each deity is a different expression of what is essentially the same nature—pristine awareness—just as electricity, though always the same, can be used in different ways: to create warmth, light, or combustion. The essence of all deities is the same pristine awareness, but because of the varying needs and inclinations of individual practitioners, they arise in various forms—with different colors, postures, expressions, implements, and adornments—and manifest different kinds of activities—pacifying, increasing, magnetizing, or wrathful.

QUESTION: Does it matter what position we sit in when we meditate?

RESPONSE: Both development and completion stage practice are supported by correct body posture. When the spine is straight, the subtle channels of the body are straight and the subtle energies can move without hindrance. This helps to make the mind clear and to keep it from jumping to outer or inner objects rather than resting in awareness. By sitting in correct posture, we create virtue and purify the body's obscurations. Recitation of mantra and prayers purifies nonvirtuous speech and enhances the qualities of pure speech. Through contemplation and other relative methods, as well as maintaining awareness of our absolute nature, we purify mind's obscurations and enhance our wisdom qualities. If we apply the three doors of body, speech, and mind simultaneously while listening to teachings and doing practice, we will quickly purify karma and accumulate both merit and wisdom.

QUESTION: There is so much to learn, understand, and contemplate in Vajrayana Buddhism. Why is it so complicated?

RESPONSE: We need a complicated method to antidote our complicated minds, filled with concepts and doubts. To put it another way, we need a medicine as complicated as our illness. With Vajrayana methods we cut through our habits, purify obscurations, and accumulate merit simultaneously.

Which practice you do depends on how you want to travel the spiritual path. If you live in California and want to go to New

York, a bicycle can get you there. It's relatively simple to make, simple to operate, and simple to repair. But if you want to go more rapidly, you can take an automobile. It's more complicated to make, operate, and repair, but it will get you there faster. Of course, you can also take an airplane. It's even more complicated to make, operate, and repair, but it will get you where you are going very quickly.

The Vajrayana is a complex path with many methods for removing confusion and delusion, but it's called the lightning path because it's so swift and direct. If you follow this path diligently, you can attain enlightenment in one lifetime or less.

QUESTION: Do we need to learn and practice all the Vajrayana methods?

RESPONSE: Ideally you would begin with the preliminary practices under the guidance of a qualified lama and follow that lama's instructions from then on. Any one of the Vajrayana practices, if undertaken diligently, will produce enlightenment. You can do only one practice, as long as you do it perfectly. Alternatively, you can pursue a number of practices.

The decision you make depends on your goal. If you aspire to help others using these methods, you need to learn as much as possible; otherwise, you can only share the few practices you know with those with whom you have a strong karmic connection. If you have learned and practiced as much as possible, you will have more methods at your disposal. A qualified teacher who upholds all the methods and lineages is like a treasure trove. He can answer any questions students may have and can provide a method for each of them based on their needs.

If you don't have that goal but undertake strong practice in just one category of the Vajrayana, you can still achieve enlightenment.

QUESTION: I've been practicing for a while, but I find it very difficult to transform my mind. Sometimes I get discouraged.

RESPONSE: Our habits have been reinforced over many lifetimes, so when we start to practice they won't change immediately. To reveal the nature of mind, the goal of Vajrayana, we need to remove our ignorance. The antidote to ignorance is wisdom, which we cultivate by listening to, contemplating, and meditating upon the teachings. Through all of this, we are skillfully guided by the teacher, and we must in turn skillfully follow the teacher's instructions. In the process, our habits will change.

Although Vajrayana is a very swift path, at first our progress may seem slow. But if we are diligent, we will gradually tame and train the mind, and the transformation will become apparent. The very fact that you realize how much work you have to do shows that you have made progress. If you have acknowledged that there is a problem, have sought solutions, and are applying methods, that *is* progress.

Sometimes in meditation your mind may seem worse than it has ever been. But that's not really so. Your mind has always been like this—you've just never noticed it. Being aware of it now is the first step in spiritual practice. If you keep going and meditate diligently, you will experience change.

Your practice won't be the same each day. Sometimes it will seem to be working; other times it will seem as though nothing at all is happening. But by consistently applying the methods, you will overcome your shortcomings and your positive qualities will become apparent. These are infallible signs that your practice is progressing.

When we start practicing, it seems as though we're trying to remove a mountain of negative karma and habit patterns with a teaspoon; we don't feel we're making much progress. But there is a Tibetan saying that, with diligence, one can even move mountains. Actually, when we use the methods of the Vajrayana, we're not using a spoon. We're leveling the mountain with a bulldozer.

17

Faith

ONCE THERE WAS an old man who went each summer with his family to a certain mountaintop to raise sheep and yaks. Many people passed his family's tent, and he always asked where they were traveling. They invariably replied, "We're going to Dodrup Chen Rinpoche to receive the direct transmission of the three verses."

One summer, the old man decided that he might as well go to see the lama too. He asked one family passing through if he could join them, and they agreed. So he went off, leaving all his sheep and yaks behind.

When they arrived at the lama's home, the old man, not knowing what to do and having nothing to ask of the lama, went to the kitchen to wait and was given some food. Meanwhile, the family requested and received a short teaching from the lama, then left for home.

The old man remained for three years, helping out in the kitchen and receiving food in return, becoming like a family member to the kitchen workers. During the entire time, he never met the lama.

One day, the cooks asked the old man to take tea to the lama. For the first time, he entered the master's room. When the lama saw him, he exclaimed, "*Atsi! Atsi! Na kha ru rakshai treng wa dra shig yin*!" which means, "Oh, my! Oh, my! Your nose is like a rudraksha bead!" Indeed, the old man's nose was very large and rough.

The old man thought to himself, "That's it, I've finally received the three-verse transmission from the lama!" He returned to his village, chanting day and night, "*Atsi! Atsi! Na kha ru rakshai treng wa dra shig yin*," counting the recitations on his prayer beads. The village people had great faith in him because, after all, he'd stayed with the lama for three years. They thought he must surely have developed extraordinary qualities. Whenever they became sick, had swelling or pain, they went to him. He blew on the affected area and they were cured. He became quite famous throughout the region.

Later, a boil that had appeared on Dodrup Chen Rinpoche's throat grew to such a size that he almost choked to death. Many doctors tried to treat him, to no avail. A visitor from the old man's area told the lama, "One of your students lives near us. He can cure you."

"Who is he?" asked the lama.

"An old man who stayed with you for three years."

"I don't remember him, but ask him to come help me."

Immediately they sent someone to fetch the old man. "You must come right away," he was told. "The lama needs help."

The old man said, "The lama gave me the three-verse transmission. I will try to help him."

Before the old man arrived, a very good cushion was brought for him to sit on, a sign of great respect. As soon as he entered the room, the lama saw his nose and remembered him, thinking, "How could this one ever heal me?"

Slowly, with one-pointed concentration, the old man began

to chant, "*Atsi, atsi . . .*" The lama burst out laughing, the boil broke open, and he was cured.

From the Vajrayana point of view, true and lasting faith has three elements. The first we might term "spiritual awe," which is what we experience if we are naturally inspired by spiritual teachings. Something about them makes our hair stand on end. Or it's what we feel when we meet a certain teacher, enter a shrine, see an image of the Buddha, or hear about his life. We experience a state of mind that is significantly different from our ordinary feelings of pleasure or happiness.

There was a great Indian scholar of the Shaivite tradition who had a powerful intellect and wrote many philosophical treatises. Once, while traveling in the Himalayas, he had a vision of the Hindu god Shiva invoking and honoring the Buddha. This made a great impression on him. Later he adopted the Buddhist religion and wrote one of the most famous prayers that the Tibetan tradition received from India, a prayer extolling the virtues of enlightenment as embodied in the Buddha Shakyamuni. Until that visionary experience, this scholar had had no faith in Buddhism. It took something deeper than a scholarly approach.

Such faith is not something we can talk ourselves—or anyone else—into. Whether we have it depends not on our intellectual sophistication but on our karma. We can't persuade someone to believe in the Buddhist teachings unless some karmic basis for belief exists. One aspect of precious human birth is having a karmic predisposition toward faith and confidence in the dharma.

Although this first element of faith is not unshakable, at least it inspires us to examine the experience and causes of suffering and how to eliminate them, and the experience and causes of happiness and how to cultivate them. The more we hear and apply the teachings, the more they resonate with our experience and the more we appreciate their truth. We are inspired to probe even more deeply, to find a teacher and follow the spiritual path. This is the second element of faith—yearning or longing to move toward the ultimate goal.

As the mind gradually opens, the teachings make more sense and we feel a connection with meditation. We need to have enough trust to follow through with our practice, and when it begins to create changes within us, that trust deepens. As the mind relaxes, we start to experience faith in and commitment to a purpose beyond changing, grinding reality. With that faith, our enthusiasm grows even more. And with more practice, we discover an uncompromising diligence. Practice reveals truth; truth liberates the poisons of the mind, freeing us to greater and greater wisdom. Each step is linked to the next. Finally we acquire a trust that is invincible. No matter what happens to us, no matter what our plight, incontrovertible faith sustains our practice until we find complete freedom: enlightenment. This is the third element of faith—the conviction that we thoroughly and profoundly understand an infallible truth.

The first element of faith, awe, is something more or less inborn. You either feel it or you don't. The second two—longing and conviction—arise from practice and can be consciously enhanced. Thus in the Vajrayana tradition, we aren't expected or even encouraged to have blind faith. True faith arises when we have heard the teachings, and applied and assimilated them until we experience infallible truth.

What we have faith in now is samsara—the world perceived with our senses. But putting our trust in worldly things won't help us in the long run, because they're all impermanent. We think we can rely on our body, but eventually it will die. We depend on outer conditions, but they are always changing. We trust our friends, but they may sour or drift away. We can only truly rely on our unchanging nature.

Suppose you have some new friends who immediately decide you're the most wonderful person in the world. Such friends may last about a week. Or they may want something from you, and they're not really your friends at all, just good actors. On the other hand, you may have friends who aren't so easy to please at first. They don't fall all over you or flash their biggest smile when they see you. But slowly, as you get to know them, you see that they are strong and true.

Having faith in samsara is like depending on a flashy friendship, one that is immediate but impermanent. To place faith in the absolute truth is to trust what is not obvious to begin with, something seemingly elusive, intangible, and inaccessible, yet in the long run the truest, steadiest object of trust. The spiritual path is not easy, for it forces us to confront just about everything we ever thought of as true or real. But if we follow through, this path will prove itself a supremely dependable friend.

QUESTION: What advice would you give someone who doesn't have a natural inclination toward devotion?

RESPONSE: To complete a task, we must be convinced that it is useful and valuable. In the same way, with spiritual practice we need to have confidence in the teacher and in the value of the teachings. We may not have great faith and devotion at first, but if we begin with that basic confidence, we can proceed. This initial faith is a sort of joy or good feeling about our connection with the teacher and the teachings, and it leads us to pursue that connection.

This type of faith can lead to a second kind—a feeling in one's heart that undertaking practice will truly bring happiness and relieve suffering. We have confidence that, through practice, our lama has gained a direct personal experience of the inner meaning of the dharma and of the means to convey it, as well as methods that will enable us to nurture that experience ourselves.

Finally, an unshakable conviction in the lama and the path arises as the benefits of practice—a lessening of our afflictive emotions, negative karma, and thus our suffering—become more and more apparent.

Those who are not naturally inclined toward devotion will realize the value of the teacher and teachings to the extent that they practice. Faith will result from practice.

18

Prayer

WHY DO WE PRAY? We might think that if we do, the Buddha or God or the deity will look kindly upon us, bestow blessings, and protect us. We might believe that if we don't, the deity won't like us and might even punish us. But the purpose of prayer is not to win the approval or avert the wrath of a God external to us.

The extent to which we understand Buddha, God, or the deity to be an expression of ultimate reality is the extent to which we receive blessings when we pray. The extent to which we have faith in the boundless qualities of the deity's love and compassion is the extent to which we receive the blessings of those qualities.

Sometimes we project human characteristics onto things that aren't human. If we sentimentally think, "My dog is meditating with me," we're merely attributing that behavior to the dog; we're imagining it. When we anthropomorphize God, we project our own faults and limitations, imagining they're God's as well. This is why many people believe that God either likes or dislikes them depending on how they behave. "I won't be able to have this or that because God doesn't like me—I forgot to pray." Or worse, "If God doesn't like me, I'll end up in hell."

If God feels happy or sad depending on whether we pray or not, then God is not flawless or an embodiment of perfect compassion and love. Any manifestation of the absolute truth, by its very nature, has neither attachment to our prayers nor aversion to our failure to pray. Such attributes are projections of our own mind.

To understand how prayer works, consider the sun, which shines everywhere without hindrance. Like God or Buddha, it continuously radiates all its power, warmth, and light without discrimination. When the earth rotates, it appears to us that the sun no longer shines. But in fact this is due to our own position on the shadowed side of the earth. If we inhabit a deep, dark mine shaft, it's not the sun's fault that we feel cold. Or if we live on the earth's surface but keep our eyes closed, it's not the sun's fault that we don't see light. The sun's blessings are all-pervasive, whether we are open to them or not. Through prayer we come out of the mine shaft, open our eyes, and make ourselves receptive to enlightened presence, the omnipresent love and compassion that exist for all beings.

Even if we aren't familiar with the idea of praying to a deity, most of us feel the presence of some higher principle or truth— some source of wisdom, compassion, and power with the ability to benefit. Praying to that higher principle will without doubt be fruitful.

However, it is very important not to be small-minded in prayer. You might want to pray for a new car, but how do you know that a new car is what you really need? It's better simply to pray for what is best, realizing that you may not know what that is. A few years ago, a Tibetan woman traveled overseas by airplane. When the plane made a brief stop en route, she got out to walk around. Unfamiliar with the airport, with the language, and with foreign travel, she didn't hear the announcement of her departing flight. This probably seemed disastrous at the time, but not long after takeoff, the plane she missed crashed and most of the passengers were killed.

We pray for what is best not only for ourselves, but for all beings. When we're starting out in practice, our self-focus is often so strong that our prayers remain very selfish and only reinforce rather than transform our self-centeredness. So until our motivation becomes more pure-hearted, it may be beneficial to spend more time cultivating loving kindness than praying.

With proper motivation, prayer becomes an important component of our practice, because it helps to dispel obstacles—counterproductive circumstances, imbalances of the body's subtle energies, and confusion and ignorance in the mind. Even when listening to the teachings, we may mentally edit what we hear, adding more than is being said or ignoring certain aspects.

The mind is like a mirror. Although our true nature is the deity, what we now experience are ordinary mind's reflections. Enemies, hindrances, inauspicious circumstances—all of which appear to be outside of us—are actually reflections of our own negativity. If you looked in a mirror and had never seen your image before, you'd think you were gazing through a window, encountering someone altogether independent of you. You would not recognize the connection. If what you saw was a horrible-looking person with a dirty face and wild hair, you might feel aversion. You might even try to clean up the image by washing the mirror. But a mirror, like the mind, is reflective—it only shows you yourself. Only if you combed your hair and washed your face could you change what you saw. You'd have to change yourself; you couldn't change the mirror. Prayer helps to purify the habits of ordinary mind and ignorance of our true nature as the deity.

When we pray in the context of deity practice, we sometimes visualize the deity standing or sitting in the space in front of us as an embodiment of perfection, separate from ourselves with our many faults and obscurations. But praying to the deity is not a matter of supplicating something separate from us. The ultimate point of using a dualistic method, visualizing the deity outside of us, is to eliminate duality.

In prayer, we visualize our inherent purity reflected as the deity and our positive qualities as the deity's form, color, and implements. This helps us to remember what already exists at the source: our perfect nature. When we visualize ourselves as the deity, we deepen our experience of our own intrinsic purity. Finally, in the completion stage of practice, when the form of the deity falls away, we let the mind rest naturally and effortlessly in its own nature, the absolute deity.

Thus we begin with an initial conception of purity as external, but then internalize it and ultimately transcend any concepts of inner and outer. This awareness of the nature of the deity increases the power, blessings, and benefit of our prayer.

If the nature of the deity is emptiness, you might wonder why we pray at all. There seems to be a contradiction: we say, on the one hand, that there really isn't a deity, only the reflection of our own intrinsic nature, but, on the other hand, we pray to the deity. This makes sense only if we understand the inseparability of absolute and relative truth.

On the absolute level, our nature is pure—we are the deity. Being unaware of this, we're bound by relative truth. To make the leap to the realization of our absolute nature, we have to walk on a relative path. Because absolute truth is so elusive to our ordinary, linear mind, we rely on an increasingly subtle, step-by-step process to work with mind's duality until we achieve recognition. Prayer is an essential part of that process.

QUESTION: I know a child whose kitten broke its leg. She prayed to the deity Tara for help. At first the kitten improved, but eventually it died and the child decided that there is no benefit to doing Tara practice. How realistic is it to expect our prayers to have an immediate effect?

RESPONSE: To explain it in a way the child could understand, we might use this example: if you have a car that isn't running well, you could reasonably expect a skilled mechanic to fix it. But if the car is completely worn out, it can't be fixed, no matter how skilled the mechanic.

What happens to a living being, whether a human or a kitten, depends on karma, as well as the immediate and incidental circumstances involved. If a kitten has the karma to sustain its body, it will live. But if the karma for living comes to an end, no amount of praying can change that. Although the child's prayers didn't seem effective, this does not mean that the practice done on the kitten's behalf was wrong or useless; it will benefit that being in a future lifetime.

People can sometimes overcome enormous obstacles through their practice, even in this lifetime, when three factors come together: faith, karma that allows for the obstacles to be overcome, and the blessings and compassion of one's object of prayer.

QUESTION: Can we actually help others through prayer and dedication of merit? If this were possible, wouldn't many people already have done so, solving all the world's problems?

RESPONSE: We definitely help others by dedicating the merit of our prayers and practice to them. However, the extent to which they will benefit is determined partly by their own receptivity. Someone who adds oil to a lamp in a dark room creates light for everyone in that room. However, those who leave the room or close their eyes won't benefit from the light. Prayer and dedication support our path because they increase our merit. The more we practice in this way, the more we become capable of helping others. Because the merit of buddhas' and bodhisattvas' prayers and dedication has accumulated over time, they can effortlessly manifest countless emanations to help an enormous number of beings. The extent to which our prayers and dedication will benefit others in the short term is determined both by their receptivity and by our own capability.

QUESTION: Is it the blessing of the deity or our sincere devotion that makes it possible to transform the mind?

RESPONSE: Both are needed; we can't have one without the other. From our own point of view, faith and devotion are most important, because they inspire us to pray and invoke the blessings of the deity, the source and object of our faith. This enables us to receive the blessings that transform our mind. Then we can attain the ultimate goal of spiritual practice—full realization of our true nature so that we can be of unceasing benefit to others.

19

Conversation with a Student

STUDENT: If the ultimate nature of experience is emptiness, what really is karma? Isn't it just a concept that's as illusory as any other?

RINPOCHE: What's involved here is the difference between absolute and relative truth. If you're not sleeping, there is no truth to the dream. Good or bad, like or dislike, sad or happy—none of it has any validity. Karma's not there at all, because the dream isn't there.

But when you're dreaming, there is good and bad, like and dislike, happy and sad, all of which create karma. If the mind is in a state of delusion, in the dream experience of relative reality, then karma is true and will make the dream better or worse. But when you awaken to ultimate reality, there is no truth to karma, to merit, or to any of it, any more than there is truth to the dream once you've awakened.

Awake, you have the *potential* to dream but you're not dreaming. It's the same with absolute truth. Relative truth is one's deluded experience of absolute truth, and within that, karma remains very powerful, merciless, accurate, and complete. Karma will determine whether we have a pleasant or an unpleasant existence, whether our rebirths are happy or sad, high or low.

STUDENT: Is it the same with the concept of merit?

RINPOCHE: Merit functions by the same process as karma, except that it involves actively working toward creating the causes of happiness in the dream of life, not only for oneself but for others.

STUDENT: With karma and merit, the same principle seems to apply: that what I put out will come back to me. This seems to imply self-centered motivation, the opposite of bodhicitta intention. Isn't it purer for a practitioner simply to remain compassionate without regard for the good karma being generated—in other words, without concern for his ultimate "reward"?

RINPOCHE: You're right to say that having compassion is better than having the ambition to make good karma so that you don't suffer. The latter is true, but only on the relative level. The teachings have different levels, and people's receptivity or perceptivity determines the most appropriate level of teaching for them. For some, a subtle seed may be planted in the mind. For others, a somewhat grosser seed must come first, to make them ready for the subtle seed. So regarding self-centered motivation versus the decision to simply be compassionate, it's true—the latter remains the ultimate choice.

STUDENT: In terms of practice, then, does merit come down to compassion in all things? Is this the essence of bodhicitta intention?

RINPOCHE: Compassion is only part of bodhicitta. The difference between bodhicitta and a lack of it depends on whether one has the aspiration to attain enlightenment for the benefit of others. If you act as if you're trying to help others, but your heart isn't really in the attainment of enlightenment for others' benefit, that isn't bodhicitta. Compassion is the impetus for doing whatever needs to be done. You aspire to attain enlightenment because you realize that you don't have the power to be of much help now.

Recognizing the suffering of beings in samsara, generating pure thoughts and compassion, aspiring to attain enlightenment in order to liberate beings, and doing everything you can to benefit others temporarily and ultimately is all relative bodhicitta. It is all activity within the dream that leads toward waking up from the dream. Absolute bodhicitta means recognizing the absolute truth beyond extremes and maintaining that recognition until it is fully obvious. That is when we awaken from the dream.

STUDENT: If the absolute nature of reality is buddhahood, shared by all beings, why doesn't everyone realize this already? What has caused the lapse into ignorance and obscuration? Is there an evolutionary principle at work, beginning in ignorance and moving on to higher consciousness?

RINPOCHE: It's not a matter of having had it once and then having forgotten it. Inherent but hidden within raw ore is gold, and extracting it requires a smelting process. Impurities are refined away until all that is left is the gold in its pure essence. Basically, a practitioner removes all of the mind's impurities to reveal the essence. It wasn't once realized and then forgotten. It's always been there but never recognized.

The difference between buddhahood and samsaric existence lies in the recognition or nonrecognition of one's true nature.

The essence is either known or not. That's the only difference. Samsara is not an evolutionary process. Delusion is not evolutionary. Realization takes place through the revelation of something inherent.

STUDENT: So the idea of a person's consciousness evolving over lifetimes is a fantasy?

RINPOCHE: Yes. Consciousness does not evolve over lifetimes. We are in the midst of the ongoing flow of samsaric existence. But as humans we have the peak opportunity for attaining buddhahood.

I suppose in a sense you could consider the bodhisattva path evolutionary, because it involves relative progress toward buddhahood. Once a person is able to see through samsara, that realization never goes away. On that basis, we walk the bodhisattva path. But it is more like evolving inwardly toward realization of one's true nature, having gone so far out into delusion. What the idea of spiritual evolution forgets to take into consideration is "de-evolution." Every sentient being goes both up and down. The process is cyclical, not evolutionary. The evolutionary theory has a lot of hope in it, but in samsara there is not much hope.

STUDENT: Then ultimately our perception of time as linear is an illusion?

RINPOCHE: Again, it's like a dream. If the mind is in the relative dream context, time exists. If the mind awakens to the absolute truth, time is nonexistent. But dream after dream, samsaric experience continues to cycle.

STUDENT: How does the practitioner know that a particular visualization is not just more of the same noisy mental activity, but rather transcends it?

It's as if practice is like looking out a full-length window and painting what you see on a canvas; you duplicate the scene, and when you're done you wipe it away. What is the difference between looking at the scene while re-creating it on the canvas, and opening the window and walking out? In other words, when does practice become realization?

RINPOCHE: Suppose a person sees a rope on the floor but thinks it's a snake; his reaction will be based on his belief that it is a snake. Though that isn't really true, his perception that it is can affect those around him. Suddenly, they all think there's a snake on the floor. It becomes so real that it even seems to slither around. The fear, reaction, and whole framework of the delusion become full-blown. But if someone comes along and says, "That's not a snake," everyone is greatly relieved. The lie has been exposed. They can see the rope as it is, as it always has been. Their delusion manipulated their perception. Those with very strong habits might see a snake again the next time they look, even though they've been told otherwise.

We use visualization to counteract this tendency to fall back into old habits. We purify distorted perceptions by visualizing phenomena purely, as the deity and the pureland. We learn how to see the snake differently until finally we recognize the rope.

A few extremely fortunate beings with very refined capabilities don't have to practice visualization. They're freed immediately upon being introduced to the nature of mind. Their delusion is like a cloud blown away by the wind. When it's gone, it's gone forever; it doesn't manifest again. Their practice then simply involves abiding in the recognition of their true nature.

We take two different tacks in order to attain realization. One involves visualization practice, because our habits lie very deep. Even though we are introduced to our absolute nature, our initial recognition doesn't stick. Visualization is a process of unlearning what we have learned and untying the knots of our ignorance. But if we don't need that process, we take the other tack and go directly to the highest path, the Great Perfection—simply resting in nondual awareness as all delusion disperses. Pure phenomena are revealed to be the display of one's absolute nature. A Great Perfection practitioner never has to paint on the canvas but steps directly out of the window.

STUDENT: So emptiness gives rise to the appearance of the deity?

RINPOCHE: All form is the deity; all form is in essence emptiness arising as appearance. The deity isn't just a being sitting on a lotus; the deity is emptiness arising as form. This means that everything in our world, including our enemies, is the deity. When someone tries to hurt us, it's hard for us to remember that, so we revert to old habits. That is why we use visualization. It's a relative method for awakening to absolute truth, but absolute truth actually appears in the form of this relative method. Comprehending more fully what we talked about earlier—the difference between absolute and relative truth, and the workings of karma within relative truth—will help you to understand more about visualization.

STUDENT: And, as a consequence, the movement toward realization?

RINPOCHE: Realization is not something grandiose. Rather, it is like penetrating something to sense or taste its essence. It's the difference between trying to describe "sweet" and experiencing sugar on your tongue. Realization is a manner of experiencing, of tasting. Meditation is the path of continuing, of keeping at it, of allowing a transformative alchemy to occur.

There are several steps to the process. As you begin to wonder about reality, questioning what is true, you see that many people accept phenomenal reality at face value. When you realize this, you feel compassion for them. Out of compassion, you pray to the lama. The lama is the source of your realization, the source of your practice. Realization has no limitation, so there is no separation between the lama and the deity. As your practice matures, so will your understanding of the lama. The lama is the deity; the lama is the truth.

You pray to the lama for clarity, strength of practice, inspiration, motivation, or whatever you need under the lama's umbrella of blessing. Then you visualize the deity. If it's a struggle, if it doesn't work or makes you grumpy, just drop it and relax. Let the mind be. Then, when thoughts resurface, try visualizing again. If you find it difficult to envision all the details, just focus on one aspect of the visualization or on your own form as an intangible, luminous body of light. Or just imagine that the deity is the embodiment of compassion and wisdom, the absolute truth.

Don't be too hard on yourself. When you can't visualize,

remember that your tenacious habits are what make you see reality as you do. Accept your difficulties, then just go on. Don't stop whenever you come to a pothole. Just go around or jump over it. A good practitioner is indomitable. Say to yourself, "Of course I have faults and shortcomings; of course I'm impatient and lazy." But then go on. Take little steps, big steps—it doesn't matter, as long as you go forward.

20

Preparing for Death

DEATH AWAITS US ALL, whether or not we're prepared, whether or not we choose to think about it. For many of us, the thought of dying engenders such uneasiness that we prefer to avoid it completely. We might even fool ourselves into believing we're not afraid of death, that it's not such a big deal. But those who die without preparation are gripped by a tremendous fear unlike anything they've ever experienced. The lack of power over the body and the loss of everything familiar brings not only disorientation and confusion, but terror. Some people feel great regret, a sense that their lives and all their efforts have been without purpose. They feel deep sadness in looking back and discovering they've missed the point of it all.

We need to prepare for the moment when the mind and body separate by developing strong habits of spiritual practice that won't evaporate in the face of death. A Tibetan aphorism says, "When you've got to go, it's too late to build a latrine." If we become familiar with the process of dying, we won't be taken by surprise, paralyzed by fear, or distracted by confusion. With the necessary meditative skill, death can be a door to the deathless state of enlightenment whereby we ceaselessly benefit all beings.

When the elements that comprise the physical body remain in balance, we stay healthy. The earth element relates to flesh and bones, the water element to blood and other bodily fluids, the fire element to digestion and heat, and the different winds to the breath, circulation, and binding of mind to body. If the balance of elements is tipped, however, with one becoming more dominant than the others, we fall ill. We might find signs of approaching death in our dreams. Dreams of being naked, headed in a southerly direction, riding an ox or a donkey, following the setting sun, veering downward, or repeatedly meeting and talking with those who have already died—all indicate some weakening of the life force.

Vajrayana practice, especially long-life practice, can be very effective for purifying the karma that causes illness and for accumulating merit—creating the positive conditions necessary to prolong life. If you aren't familiar with such meditation, you can create great merit by saving animals that would otherwise be killed. You might buy all the live fish and worms in a bait shop and set them free, motivated by the compassionate understanding that no being wants to die, that each values its existence, and that great virtue comes from saving a life. Dedicate the virtue you create to all who are experiencing obstacles to long life and pray that these obstacles will be removed. Do this repeatedly. If your dream signs don't change, it means that the karma sustaining your life is coming to an end and that death is not far away.

When you are seriously ill, the sense faculties begin to fail. Unless you are familiar with your mind's true nature, this is a very frightening and confusing time, for all you have ever relied upon to orient yourself falls away. Your vision becomes cloudy, appearances seem mirage-like and unstable, and visionary experiences may arise. Your body feels heavy, as if it were sinking into the bed.

At death, the elements lose their power. They no longer support one another, and the mind separates from the body. When the elements begin to disassociate, the ability to conceptualize and to differentiate between self and other, subject and object, diminishes. The male energy residing at the crown of the head descends, the female energy in the navel rises, and the two join in the heart. All thoughts cease, and you fall into a death swoon, a coma-like state. Subsequently, you experience unobstructed awareness, or "clear light"; this is the first stage of the *chönyid bardo,* the bardo of the true nature of reality.

The term "clear light" denotes clarity: the absence of delusion, subject–object duality, dullness, and concepts. It refers to open awareness and is also called "foundational clear light" because it is the basic nature of all beings. It doesn't refer to what people who have had near-death experiences describe: a brilliant light to which they are drawn, a voice saying, "You have to go back now." Clear light doesn't have anything to do with physical light.

If we are skilled at resting in awareness, we can find liberation in the chönyid bardo by recognizing clear light as none other than our own nature. Blending our awareness with clear light produces dharmakaya liberation.

If we don't have sufficient meditation, clear light arises like a flash of lightning and is gone. Unfamiliar with the true nature of mind, we are unable to use this brief transition to attain enlightenment.

Next the pure, unceasing qualities of the open nature of mind arise in a vivid display of peaceful and wrathful deities, the second stage of the chönyid bardo. If we recognize these phenomena as none other than the radiance of our intrinsic awareness, this transition becomes an opportunity to attain sambhogakaya liberation. If, however, we have no understanding of how the mind projects appearances, we won't recognize this display for what it is. It will be like momentarily catching sight of our shadow but not recognizing it.

If our practice of the Great Perfection paths of *trekchöd* and *tögal* has been strong, we can find liberation in one of these two stages of the chönyid bardo. Otherwise, these opportunities for liberation elude us, and the mind's duality takes form as the experience of self and other, the process of ordinary sentience in samsara.

We enter the *sipa bardo,* or bardo of becoming, the forty-nine-day transition to rebirth. At first everything seems as it did in our human life. We still perceive our home, the people we love. Because we no longer have a corporeal body, they don't know we're there. We hear everything they say, but they can't hear us. To complicate matters, we may not know we're dead. We might sit down at the table with our family and wonder why no one passes us any food. We may not understand why no one responds when we ask a question. This brings unbearable sadness. And once we figure out that we've died, great fear arises.

The sipa bardo includes four stages marked by terrifying sounds and three stages of fearful experiences of the environment. Our consciousness, unfettered by a physical body, is buffeted about. Any arising thought instantaneously propels us to its object. If in life we develop strong faith and a habit of praying when things seem beyond hope, no matter what our spiritual tradition, we will remember to pray at this time. The power of prayer is far greater in the sipa bardo than it is in this human realm, where we are bound by our corporeal body. The moment we think of our source of refuge, we will be reborn in that wisdom being's pure realm. This is nirmanakaya liberation. If we don't find liberation at this point, the mind will move into another dream, taking rebirth in one of the six realms, having lost all the opportunities to awaken, to find rebirth beyond suffering.

Through the great practice of *p'howa,* or transference of consciousness, we can project our consciousness at the time of death to a pure realm of experience such as that of the Buddha Amitabha or a particular deity. Unlike a god realm, a pureland is the display of one's inherent purity, a realm of infinite bliss. Those who have attained such rebirth know no suffering and eventually attain enlightenment.

Called the "meditation of nonmeditation" because it is relatively easy to accomplish, p'howa is widely taught in the Vajrayana tradition. Within only one or two weeks of practicing "p'howa of the three recognitions," one of five kinds of p'howa, we can develop the ability to direct our consciousness at death. Signs of accomplishment appear, indicating that the channels of the subtle body are no longer blocked and that our consciousness will be easily transferred through the crown of the head to a pureland. This practice is like a bridge linking dharma from this life to the next.

In a pureland, we receive teachings from a buddha and meditate, purifying our remaining karma and opening the door to realization. We won't return to samsara by the force of our karma, but will have the power to intentionally incarnate in order to benefit those still trapped. For beginners as well as those too busy to do other spiritual practices and attain liberation in this lifetime, p'howa provides a safety net, a means of ensuring that, at death, their consciousness will not be dominated by the winds of karma.

Some Vajrayana practitioners don't need to rely on formal p'howa practice because of the strength of their development and completion stage meditation. At the close of the development stage, we visualize the entire universe resolving into the seed syllable of the deity, which itself disappears into emptiness. Then during the completion stage, we abide in the nature of mind. Finally, we once again recognize all form, sound, and thought as the body, speech, and mind of the deity. The practice of maintaining this awareness of vajra body, speech, and mind consistently throughout our lives can produce liberation in the bardo.

If you are dying and aren't familiar with Vajrayana or don't have confidence in your practice, visualize that whoever you have enduring faith in—your lama if you are a Buddhist practitioner —is inseparable from the Buddha Amitabha, surrounded by his retinue in the pureland, seated a forearm's length above the crown of your head. Due to our delusion, we would not normally perceive a pure realm at death, for the inherent purity of experience becomes apparent only when the obscurations masking that purity have been removed. However, even if visualization is difficult, we focus at death on the Buddha Amitabha as the expression of perfection, because his commitment is that whoever hears his name or prays to him, no matter how nonvirtuous, will eventually find rebirth in his pureland, Dewachen.

Every day until you die, with the Buddha Amitabha as your witness, confess and purify all of the nonvirtue you've created in this and all previous lives. Dedicate all of the virtue you've accumulated to the benefit of all beings. Pray that at the time of death, without any other rebirth intervening, you and all beings will find rebirth in Amitabha's pureland, receive teachings directly from Amitabha, undertake practice, and attain enlightenment.

If you're not a practicing Buddhist or are unfamiliar with the Buddha Amitabha's appearance, you can focus on the space above the crown of your head. There are two advantages to doing this. First, by focusing elsewhere, you distract yourself from your pain and fear. Second, your consciousness can leave the physical body through any one of nine "doors," each leading to a different rebirth. Eight finger widths back from the original hairline, at the crown of your head, lies the door to rebirth in a pureland. In the days before you die and at the time of death, focus on this spot, visualizing your mind merging with space. Even if you don't achieve rebirth in a pureland, you won't be born in a lower realm.

If you are helping a dying person—a non-Buddhist—you can describe this visualization practice. But you will only create confusion and make things more difficult if you start talking in Buddhist terms when death is imminent. Instead, support the person by suggesting that she visualize the object of her faith above the crown, praying at death to join that wisdom being in heaven or whatever she considers to be a pure realm. At the moment of death, tap the crown of her head. This will bring the consciousness to the door leading to the pureland. Don't touch any other part of the body, for that will draw the consciousness to a lower door and possibly a lower rebirth.

It is very helpful to encourage relatives and loved ones to leave before the moment of death. They should say what they wish and then bid their good-byes. Otherwise, their attachment to the dying person or her attachment to them might prove distracting, and instead of concentrating on the visualization of the source of refuge or the space above the crown, she will focus on them.

If the dying don't let go of their attachments to the ones they love and the objects they cherish, their minds may be caught by these attachments after death and they may become what we call ghosts. And though they won't intend to harm, their consciousness will hover in the human realm and be felt as discomfort or illness by those they've left behind. Focusing above the crown, on the Buddha Amitabha or another source of refuge, helps to draw attention away from such attachments.

No matter what your age, it is very important to write a will. If you die without one, you may cling to your possessions, possibly leading to rebirth as a hungry ghost. You will also miss the benefit of having given your things away; offering your belongings to others is an act of generosity that creates virtue.

In addition to providing for the support of your family and children in your will, you can also leave something to those who are hungry or sick, or to practitioners. In Buddhism there is a tradition that may exist in other religions as well: that of making offerings to monasteries on behalf of those who are sick or who have died. During daily services, prayers are offered for all of those who, since its founding, have had a connection to the monastery through their faith, prayers, and offerings of effort, substance, or financial support. All of this merit is continuously dedicated, producing a great multiplication of virtue and long-term benefit. If you leave a donation to a monastery or church in your will, before you die dedicate this virtue to all beings.

If you haven't prepared a will, even if you can no longer speak or write, you can formulate a dedication in your mind: "To whoever needs or wants it, I give everything I've accumulated in order to benefit all beings." This act of generosity, too, will create virtue.

It is crucial to begin preparing for death now, whether you are young or old, healthy or sick. Begin by reflecting on impermanence. Each night when you go to bed, remind yourself that this day may have been your last—you may not awaken in the morning. Then review your life and think about its purpose. Reflect on the fact that death is the greatest of all transitions. Visualizing the Buddha Amitabha or the wisdom being in whom you have faith, recall the nonvirtue you've created and purify your wrongdoing by invoking the four powers of support, regret, commitment, and blessing. Also reflect on the practice you've done and the ways you've been helpful, and dedicate the merit to every being. If you haven't yet bequeathed your worldly possessions, mentally give them away to whoever might need them without clinging to anything. Then dedicate this merit to every being with the wish that samsaric suffering cease, that all might awaken to their true nature. Pray that you and others will go directly, without any other rebirth intervening, to a pureland. Or, if you're not a Buddhist, pray that you and all beings will attain after death whatever state you believe lies beyond painful existence.

Then imagine your death—a car wreck, a heart attack, or the misery of cancer. Imagine how it would feel to be carried away in an ambulance, hearing the doctor say, "There is nothing left to do." Fear and overwhelming helplessness will arise. You will experience attachment to your family, sense the futility of your life, and feel the suffering of impending death. Then say to yourself, "I am dying. Clinging to my family or my money won't give me one second more. Everyone dies. The greatest spiritual masters and most powerful beings down to the tiniest insects have come and gone. Death is a transition, just as is this dream called life. I've experienced both many times before. Now at least I have methods that will help me. Most people aren't so fortunate. This time death is an opportunity for liberation."

Contemplating repeatedly this way can give rise to great inspiration and rejoicing.

Before you go to sleep, clearly imagine the object of your faith above your head. Pray that, upon death, by the power of your accumulated virtue and the blessings of that wisdom being, you and all beings will attain rebirth in a pure realm. Then visualize your consciousness moving out through the crown of your head to join inseparably with the heart essence of the wisdom being above you.

Such preparation not only helps to reduce fear and anguish and increase your meditative capability at the time of death; it also increases your appreciation for your precious human birth and reinforces your aspiration to use whatever time remains to create the greatest benefit for yourself and others. You can complete this nightly contemplation by praying, "If I awaken tomorrow, I will commit myself to using my body, speech, and mind fully to practice and to help others." Even if half or three-quarters of your life has passed and you haven't yet made this commitment, you can still do so now.

Many people worry that if they spend too much time thinking about death, they'll invite it. Yet poor people often dream about becoming rich, and hungry people about food; that neither makes them rich nor fills their stomachs. No matter how much we might imagine living for a long time, we may still die young. It's not true that we hasten death by preparing for it.

Throughout the day remind yourself that death isn't far away. All it takes is a small blood clot lodging in your brain or a car running a red light. Although it may make you uncomfortable, the more you ponder this, the less fearful you will be.

At the time of death, your consciousness revisits all the places you've ever been. So during this life, wherever you go, practice praying to the lama, the deity, or some other source of refuge that by the power of their blessings you and all beings may find rebirth in a pureland. When your consciousness returns to these places at death, your memory of having prayed there will lead you to pray again and you will instantly awaken in a pureland.

Whatever you do, whatever happens to you, remind yourself that your experience is illusory. Practice recognizing, "This is a dream; there is nothing solid or permanent to it. This is the bardo." Pray to your object of faith that you will be liberated. If you establish this habit well before death, you will remember this meditation and prayer in the bardo.

You can evaluate what the probable strength of your meditation will be at the time of death by watching your dreams. If you remain in mind's clear light—no longer involved with ordinary dream phenomena, but resting in awareness of your true nature—your practice is very great and death will be the door to liberation. If you usually have dream recognition—if you are aware while dreaming that you're in the dream state—then when you encounter death, you'll most likely maintain some control over the situation. If you are caught up in your dreams, responding, for example, to a dream-enemy with anger rather than compassion, your emotions may determine the nature of your after-death experience. If you are doubtful about your meditative capability, now is the time to strengthen it through practice.

By preparing throughout your life—with contemplation of impermanence and the illusory, dreamlike nature of experience, prayer, development and completion stage practice, p'howa, and the Great Perfection practice of resting in awareness of mind's nature—you can transform the fear and anguish of death and dying into an opportunity for profound spiritual practice and ultimate freedom.

QUESTION: If we don't find liberation at death, how much of the practice we've done in this life will we retain in the next?

RESPONSE: Two aspects of karma are relevant here. "Behavior in harmony with the initial action" means that the spiritual qualities you have developed in this life—such as faith, love, and compassion—will be evident from an early age in your next. "Experience according directly with the initial action" means that if you undertake spiritual practice but don't attain enlightenment in this lifetime or liberation in the bardo, you will have at least established a habit of meditation. That pattern will create a similar opportunity in your next life.

QUESTION: Could you please talk more about the bardos? I'm confused about what they really are.

RESPONSE: The Tibetan word *bardo* refers to six intermediate states of experience. During the first three, which take place in this life, one can prepare for death, during or after which the other three occur. The Tibetan *kye nay bardo* refers to the intermediate state between birth and death, the bardo of this lifetime. Of the six bardos, this is the most important. It is here that we can choose either to create happiness for ourselves and others in this and future lives, or to become more deeply mired in the cycles of suffering and cause others to do the same. If we use the opportunity afforded by the bardo of this lifetime to create virtue and refrain from nonvirtue, we can ensure more fortunate experiences in future lifetimes and avoid feeling regret at the time of death.

Within this bardo are two additional intermediate states—the meditation bardo and the dream bardo. Meditation methods applied in these three bardos help us derive the greatest benefit from the three bardos of the transition of death.

The meditation bardo, called the *samten bardo,* extends from the beginning to the end of a meditation session. Ideally, we make this life's bardo as much of a meditation bardo as we can in order to prepare for death. We develop the caliber of practice necessary to help us deal with the difficulties of this lifetime as well as death and the after-death experience.

The dream bardo, or *milam bardo,* takes place from the time we go to sleep to the time we awaken. Instead of wasting eight or nine hours a day sleeping, we can use this time for dream yoga. Our daytime and nighttime practices then support each other. During the day, we practice recognizing the illusory quality of our experience. Looking back, we see that all of our life's experiences, which once seemed so substantial and true, are now nothing more than memories. We recognize that all circumstances—whether we are being praised or blamed, whether we are happy or sad—are dreamlike. Then our meditation will bear fruit at night, and we will recognize that we are dreaming. The more we realize the dreamlike nature of our lives, the less attachment and suffering we will experience at death, and the more we will be able to apply meditative methods at the time of death.

The meditative skill that we develop in the three bardos of this lifetime can enable us to use the three bardos of the dying and after-death process as doorways to enlightenment.

The bardo of the moment of death begins when the conditions that will cause our death—for instance, a terminal illness—first arise and lasts until the elements of the body cease functioning.

If we are accomplished in the practice of p'howa, we can direct our consciousness at the moment of death to a pure realm, from which we can benefit beings suffering in samsara and continue our path to enlightenment under superb conditions. If we have practiced advanced methods such as the Great Perfection, we may recognize the first or second stage of the chönyid bardo, and the "child clear light," the awareness that we have maintained through our meditation, will merge with the "mother clear light," the absolute nature of mind. Their union is our enlightenment.

If we haven't practiced in the bardo of this lifetime, we will miss these opportunities for liberation, and the mind will move into the next intermediate state, the sipa bardo, or the bardo of becoming. This is the interval between the dissolution of the chönyid bardo and the beginning of the next samsaric rebirth. The sipa bardo is what most people mean when they refer to "the bardo." When we pray in the sipa bardo, we merge with the object of our prayer and are reborn in a pure realm of experience.

PART V

On the Vajrayana Path

21

Guru Yoga

THE BUDDHA SAID, "Without the lama, there would be no buddhas." Many of the Buddhist scriptures and commentaries state that, before the advent of the teacher in one's life, not even the concept of enlightenment exists, let alone the determined search for it. All spiritual methods, starting with the initial steps of taking refuge and bodhisattva vows, come from the lama.

In one way we have great fortune: we're living in an eon blessed by the appearance of a thousand buddhas, of which the Buddha Shakyamuni is the fourth. But in another way we are unfortunate, for none of these buddhas has manifested in our time. However, as the Buddha Shakyamuni passed into parinirvana and his retinue implored him to remain, he promised that in periods of spiritual degeneration he would appear in the form of spiritual teachers, that the dissolution of his nirmanakaya form would not hamper his activity in any way; the benefit would be the same.

Relying on a teacher to achieve liberation is the essence of the practice called guru yoga. *Guru* is the Sanskrit term for lama, or spiritual teacher. The Tibetan word for the Sanskrit *yoga* is *naljor; nalwa* means "pure nature" and *jor* means "to attain." Through guru yoga the lama's realization of mind's pure nature dawns as realization in our own mindstreams.

Understanding that the lama is the union of all sources of refuge speeds our progress on the path. If we relied solely on the yidam, for example, we would reach our goal far more slowly. The meditational deity is only one of the outer, inner, and secret sources of refuge all contained in the body, speech, and mind of the lama.

The lama embodies the Three Jewels of Buddha, dharma, and sangha; the Three Roots of lama, yidam, and dakini; the wealth deity; the dharma protectors; and the three kayas.

The mind of the lama, the lama's realization of absolute truth, is identified with the buddha principle of the Three Jewels. The speech of the lama embodies the dharma principle, the transmission of the teachings that benefit all who receive them. The body of the lama is the principle of the sangha and the enactment of virtuous activity that leads beings to liberation.

In addition, the physical form of the teacher embodies the first of the Three Roots, the lama as the source of blessings. Though we don't have the karma to have received teachings directly from the Buddha Shakyamuni, the lama speaks as the Buddha would have spoken and uses the means to guide us that the Buddha would have used.

We receive the lama's blessings directly through empowerment, instruction, and guidance in our practice. The lama introduces us to the fact that cyclic existence is a state of suffering, to the necessity of gaining liberation from that suffering, and to the means of doing so.

After hearing and applying the lama's teachings, we begin to experience renunciation: we turn away from thoughts and actions that are counterproductive to spiritual development and cultivate those that are productive. Where there was ignorance, we now have some understanding. Where there was only ordinary conceptual mind, we now taste awareness. Our mind's poisons and pervasive self-interest slowly diminish, and our ability to deal with them increases. Our perception of the world begins to change. These are all blessings of the lama.

Just as the physical form of the lama embodies the root of blessings, so does the lama's speech embody the principle of the yidam as the root of accomplishment. The Sanskrit term for accomplishment is *siddhi;* the Tibetan is *ngödrup.* On the most profound level, these terms refer to realization of the true nature of mind. So far the only thing we have accomplished is the failure to recognize this nature and thus the perpetuation of samsara.

However, realization of our true nature, not samsara, is the accomplishment we rightly seek. By ripening us through empowerment, freeing us through teachings, and sustaining our practice with blessings and inspiration, the lama enables us to experience that nature directly. Yidam means "mental commitment"—a commitment to listen to and apply unerringly the methods given us by the lama. By keeping this commitment, we realize the ultimate accomplishment. Thus we say that the lama's speech, the lama's teaching, is inseparable from the yidam.

The mind of the lama embodies the third of the Three Roots —the dakini, the feminine principle of wisdom and the root of auspicious circumstances and enlightened activity. When awareness of the true nature of phenomena has become an ongoing state of realization, auspicious circumstances and enlightened activity manifest without effort, as a natural outflow.

We usually refer to four kinds of enlightened activity: pacification, enrichment, the activity of power, and direct wrathful intervention. On the relative level, pacification means allaying one's fears and suffering. Enrichment means increasing one's merit, longevity, and health in this lifetime. Power means drawing together the necessary circumstances to support spiritual development. Direct wrathful intervention means quickly cutting through obstacles on the path.

Each of these activities also has a more profound function. The ultimate activity of pacification resolves the poisons of the mind, including ignorance concerning the nature of reality, in their own ground. Ultimate enrichment brings the accumulations of merit and wisdom to full expression. The ultimate activity of power overcomes all confused and superficial thought patterns through awareness of their true nature. Finally, ultimate direct wrathful intervention annihilates all the ways in which we invest things with a self-nature and solidity they do not have; the sword of transcendent knowledge cuts through and liberates ignorance.

The teacher embodies yet another principle, that of the wealth deity. In Vajrayana Buddhism there are wealth deities and practices. Many people believe that if they do such practices they will become rich. Actually, another kind of enrichment takes place: that of merit, aspiration, and spiritual qualities in daily life. One of the effects of these practices may very well be material prosperity, but that is only incidental to the major benefit of releasing the mind from avarice and greed. The lama is the source of methods by which we accumulate merit and break the tight bonds of selfish desire and insatiability. This helps us to become free of both material and spiritual poverty. Thus the lama is said to be inseparable from the wealth deity.

The lama also embodies the principle of the dharma protectors (in Sanskrit, *dharmapalas*). The Tibetan term for protector is *gonpo,* which means guide or ally, someone who helps or benefits. Although traditional depictions of dharma protectors as wrathful and ferocious beings with large mouths, heads, and eyes have symbolic value, the underlying meaning remains that of an ally, the supportive influence of the teacher and the teachings. Ultimately, it is our own path of virtue that protects us from the suffering we would otherwise experience as a result of nonvirtue. But it is the teacher who instructs us in the consequences of nonvirtue and the benefits of virtue. The lama safeguards our dharma practice, protecting us from any misunderstanding of the teachings or errors in applying them.

Finally, the lama embodies the three kayas. The mind of the lama is dharmakaya, original purity beyond confusion and delusion. The lama's realization of the formless, substanceless nature beyond words is transmitted nonverbally from mind to mind. The speech of the lama is sambhogakaya, that which is halfway apparent or intangible. The physical body of the lama is the nirmanakaya display of enlightened mind, appearing in tangible form to show us the path, to guide and lead us to liberation.

We can't devise infallible spiritual methods on our own. Life is very short: we don't have time to waste reinventing the wheel. Nor can we learn methods from books alone, for what we get from reading is highly subjective—we give it our own interpretation. A book can't offer us feedback like, "No, wait a minute, that's not what I meant," so we have no way of verifying our understanding.

Words and concepts can't liberate us, for they are part of the mechanism of dualistic mind. They can't give us a taste of mind's essence or lead us to its realization. Even the enlightened Buddha said, "Though I would think to say, there are no words." Given the limitations of human intelligence and conceptual thinking, it is impossible to communicate the absolute truth verbally. Conceptual mind is bound by subject–object duality. But mind's true nature cannot be grasped dualistically; it is self-knowing.

Though words can't catch the absolute truth, they can point to it. Like a finger pointing to the moon, the lama's words can indicate the right direction. Ultimately, it is the teacher's realization of the truth that catalyzes the awakening to our own intrinsic awareness.

Relating to a teacher is like plugging into an electrical outlet. If electricity is flowing, it will come directly to us. But if there isn't any electricity coming through, nothing will happen. This may not be the best of examples, but in a way it's a good one because most of us don't know exactly what electricity is. We only know what it can do. By relating to one who has a direct experience of the absolute truth, we can connect with that truth. The purpose of honoring, having faith in, and being receptive to the teacher is to realize this truth ourselves, not simply to appreciate someone else's realization of it.

When our mind starts to change as a result of the methods the lama gives us, we begin to recognize more and more of the lama's noble qualities, and our faith increases. When our faith meets the realization of the lama, the meaning of the absolute nature is born in our minds. The combination of the teacher's qualities and our own faith, prayer, and practice liberates us.

Because the methods we use don't require proximity to the lama, we can practice guru yoga anywhere—even if the lama is no longer alive. If we have strong faith, we can pray to the lama in the morning about something we don't understand and gain some insight or resolution by the afternoon. This is because the lama's essence is wisdom, which, like the light of the sun, is all-pervasive, the same whether near or far. Though the sun sets, it doesn't stop shining. Through our habit of dualistic perception, we build walls in basic space, creating artificial boundaries. On the level of ultimate reality, however, there is no separation, no near or far—the lama's wisdom is no different from that of all enlightened beings. This all-pervasive wisdom that transcends one or many, separate or together, is the absolute lama.

Through the blessings of the lama and the diligent practice of guru yoga, our realization increases and a profound faith grows that brings tears to our eyes and makes our hair stand on end. Our mind opens to this same wisdom, blending in boundless space with the mind of the lama. This is the mind-to-mind lineage.

It is difficult to find a perfectly qualified teacher, but the one we choose as our guide on the spiritual path should at least have certain qualities. The teacher should not only thoroughly understand the teachings but have attained some direct realization of them, enjoying the inner warmth of meditative insight, an energy that penetrates to the heart of the Buddha's words. The teacher's practice should have reached a stage where an indwelling confidence in the deeper meaning of the teachings and the dynamic energy of realization has been attained. Such a teacher's mindstream is filled with spontaneous, unfabricated love and compassion for all beings. Seeing or hearing her, even thinking about or touching her, is beneficial. Her experience is so vast that it overflows to others. A teacher like this is someone worthy of the title "lama."

The Tibetan word *lama* refers to two essential qualities: *la* means "high," in the sense of the most sublime realization of the nature of mind; *ma* means "motherly," referring to the quality of unconditional compassion that arises from realization. Although there are thirty attributes of a qualified teacher, a lama will be of benefit if he meets the crucial criterion of possessing mother-like compassion and has students' interests completely at heart. Such a lama will have no desire for fame or a large circle of followers—only a sincere wish to bring about changes in students' minds that will produce liberation.

A lama must be familiar enough with the vast array of Buddhist methods to find the one most suitable for each individual student. Moreover, she should have a facility for working with people of different dispositions.

At the very least, a lama should function like a doctor, not necessarily the best in the world, but a good one. Just as a competent specialist who treats only one type of disease can benefit those with that particular malady, a teacher whose knowledge and experience may be limited can still be beneficial.

Teachers need to be honest about their limitations. They shouldn't pretend they know or understand something they don't and thereby mislead students who believe in them. Many teachers make a big mistake in not referring students to someone else who can help them in a particular area or better meet their needs.

Teachers with pure intention will do whatever may prove necessary—nurturing, guiding, protecting, or sending students elsewhere, displaying peaceful or wrathful means—without concern for themselves. Those with altruistic motivation who speak only of what they understand, and who maintain dignity, integrity, and ethical behavior, benefit their students even if they don't possess all the qualities of an ideal lama. However, if a teacher lacks the pure intention of bodhicitta, students will eventually sense that something is wrong. Tibetans say that a dog turd wrapped in beautiful brocade will look lovely for a while, but sooner or later somebody is going to smell it. Without pure intention, a person can act like a spiritual teacher and perhaps bring short-term benefit to a few people, but sooner or later the absence of qualities will become apparent. Problems and difficulties will develop that make it obvious something is awry. According to another Tibetan proverb, falsehood goes only as far as a guinea pig's tail—which means not very far at all. On the other hand, truth is long lasting, like a valley you can walk through for days without reaching the end. When a person's life is in harmony with the truth, positive qualities endure. Those who pretend to be teachers, fooling themselves and others, have as much to sustain their posturing as the length of a guinea pig's tail. After a while, they cease to convince anyone.

Before we accept someone as our teacher, we must carefully examine her qualities and capabilities. Although a false teacher may not have negative intent, to rely on such a person is like drinking poison. At the same time, for a teacher to accept a student without examination is like jumping off a cliff. The teacher has to determine whether the student has correct motivation and intends to apply the teachings appropriately, without distorting or corrupting them for some selfish purpose.

Once we begin to study with a qualified teacher, that teacher becomes more important to us than the Buddha Shakyamuni himself. This is because, even though the teacher's qualities could never exceed those of the Buddha, he is a living teacher, someone through whom we have direct contact with the dharma. The founders of our current healing tradition were very kind, but they are long dead. We get our medical care from living practitioners who uphold the long tradition of past healers. Likewise, the lama can help us in a more immediate, personal way than the Buddha himself and therefore is regarded as even kinder than the Buddha.

The title "Rinpoche," Tibetan for "precious" or "of inestimable value," is sometimes applied to lamas because of their significance in their students' lives. The term comes from the Indian and Tibetan mythology of the wish-fulfilling gem, a gem that appears as a result of beings' merit and aspirations and is so magical that any wish made in its presence is fulfilled. The lama is like such a gem.

When we admire and respect a lama, we want to be like her, to possess her same wonderful qualities. This inspires us to apply the teachings, confident that they will lead us to the same state she embodies. The tantras say that to depend on the lama is to rely on all buddhas; to behold the face of the lama is to behold the face of a thousand buddhas. It is said that if one sees the lama as a buddha, one will receive a buddha's blessings. If we understand that she has all the qualities of a buddha, we will follow her guidance wholeheartedly until we attain enlightenment. If we have no faith or devotion, if we remain cynical or skeptical, we won't follow through with our practice and will never progress on the path.

Devotion to the lama should not be construed as excessive, mindless dedication to someone whose intentions may be questionable, like that of a slave to his master. We feel devotion for the lama not for his sake, nor to please or make him rich, but to increase our receptivity so that waves of blessings and merit can infuse our mindstream.

What we feel is based on a deep appreciation for what the lama gives us. We understand that through her compassion, realization, and blessings, as well as our own faith, devotion, and desire to emulate those qualities, we will experience the inseparability of our mind from that of the lama.

As soon as we start to practice guru yoga with genuine devotion, we begin to notice changes. Our negative emotions and confusion diminish, and our positive qualities and realization increase. Our relationships improve; we become calmer and more relaxed, less likely to get upset or to argue with people. All of these tangible benefits reinforce our faith in the lama and the teachings. The more our faith increases, the more we feel the lama's blessings. This increases our faith even more, which increases the blessings, a process that continues until we reach a level of unchanging, incontrovertible faith. At that point our confidence is unshakable.

The relationship between student and teacher as the very foundation of the path must be properly understood. Though it has been greatly misinterpreted, it isn't something new to Buddhism or a recent innovation devised to attract students. Rather, it has been a proven method of practice for highly realized practitioners and masters over thousands of years. The reason there are lineages of genuine spiritual teachings alive today is that practitioners, generation after generation, have gone through the process of finding a true teacher, relating to that teacher with devotion and respect, receiving spiritual transmission, gaining realization, and then joining the next generation of those who inspire respect and devotion in their students. That is how it has happened in the past, and it is clearly happening now. As long as there are people willing to devote themselves to benefiting others, and as long as there are those who can advise them on the means to do so, that is how it will continue into the future.

QUESTION: In order to attain enlightenment, how much should we rely on ourselves and how much on the lama or some other external power?

RESPONSE: We need to rely on both the lama and our own efforts. Though we gain realization through our own efforts, the catalyst for this transformation is a relationship with a worthy teacher and the application of authentic teachings.

When we begin practicing, we look beyond our own limited experience for the means to liberation; it's not enough to rely entirely on ourselves, because that hasn't worked in the past. If it had, we wouldn't still be wandering in samsara. None of us wants to suffer, yet we do, despite our best efforts. So we must look to something or someone who can show us the way beyond suffering.

At the same time, we rely on our own efforts by listening carefully to the teachings, deeply contemplating their meaning, and finally internalizing them through meditation. So in the final analysis, it is mainly through our own practice that we accomplish our goal. Success lies, in a sense, in the very palm of our hand.

QUESTION: Is the lama really necessary? Is there a concept of grace in Vajrayana Buddhism?

RESPONSE: If you want to build a house but have no experience in construction, it would make sense to work with a contractor you have confidence in. If you tried to do it yourself, you might make mistakes: the house might not last very long; it might even collapse, causing great injury to yourself and others. So you investigate the background and experience of several contractors until you find someone fully qualified.

Similarly, in spiritual practice we choose a lama, an experienced guide to lead us through the stages of meditation. The path is not the same for every practitioner, nor for any one practitioner at different stages. It's like climbing stairs. We need to go step by step, relying on someone who knows the way, who can see where we are on the staircase and determine when we can take the next step.

At first we may not have faith in the lama or the teachings. That lack of faith creates an apparent division between what is "inside" and "outside" the mind. The distinction we make between self and other, as well as our lack of trust, consistently reinforces that wall of duality. Through practice and devotion for the lama, we break down the wall, allowing our own true nature to merge with the enlightened mind of the lama.

Spiritual practice is a process of inner transformation. To become enlightened, we must maintain an unwavering recognition of the nature of mind. The relationship between the lama and student provides the swiftest means of accomplishing this. If grace alone were sufficient, all beings would already be liberated, because no enlightened being would ever willingly leave anyone in a state of suffering. Just as we must expose ourselves to the sun to benefit from its warmth and light, we need to make ourselves receptive to the lama's blessings through our own effort. When that effort and the lama's blessings meet, infallible benefit arises.

QUESTION: What should I do if I have difficulty developing faith in the lama and the Buddhist teachings?

RESPONSE: In the West, in addition to a marvelous array of material resources, there is a tradition of faith and prayer. You might begin by exploring the spiritual methods of your own culture, the one you're most familiar with. If they don't offer what you seek, then try exploring the spiritual approaches of other cultures.

If in this process you discover that your purpose in following a spiritual path is to uproot the causes of suffering, to gain complete liberation for yourself, and to lead others to liberation, you need to seek out teachers and teachings that can help you.

If you want to become free in this lifetime, you need to rely on a teacher, and that teacher must be qualified. For your relationship with a teacher to be productive, you have to be able to trust him and the teachings. How do you establish that trust?

You must first understand that all teachers are human beings. Some have very good qualities—they have established pure motivation, studied well, and developed genuine personal experience and understanding of the teachings. Some are self-serving and use the spiritual path to achieve their own selfish goals. They haven't made a commitment out of deep-hearted compassion to help others reduce their suffering and to bring benefit. Some have mixed motivation and experience. So you must carefully examine a teacher's history, training, experience, and activity.

Initially, there is nothing wrong with having doubt or lacking faith. However, to proceed on the path you must at some point remove that doubt. To do so, you need to examine the teacher. It is inappropriate and a waste of time to follow a teacher's instructions before assessing her, and then to criticize her because they aren't working for you—just as it is to criticize an unexamined doctor whose regimen hasn't cured you. If you find a teacher who doesn't have the qualities you seek, then don't pursue your relationship with her. But if she does display those qualities, then you needn't look further. At that point, you must follow the teacher's instructions without delay, just as you would the recommendations of a qualified doctor once you were confident of his skills and credentials.

QUESTION: You referred to the lama's mind as the dakini, but I thought that the dakini is a female deity.

RESPONSE: Dakini refers to the feminine principle of wisdom that manifests in female form to benefit beings. We say the lama's mind is the dakini because it embodies the inseparability of emptiness and wisdom, the absolute dakini. This absolute nature, dharmakaya, manifests as the subtle display of the sambhogakaya dakini and the nirmanakaya, or physical, form of great female realization holders in order to benefit beings.

QUESTION: Is it more beneficial to study with one lama or with many?

RESPONSE: The teacher is like a doctor and the practice like medicine. You don't go to a doctor for her sake but because you need to get well. Though many doctors may come highly recommended, there is no point in visiting them all or mixing the medications they prescribe. Similarly, there is no reason to shop for spiritual teachings without ever fully applying any one of them.

If, after following a doctor's treatment plan carefully, you experience some improvement, you can augment this regimen with that of a specialist. Similarly, after choosing a reliable teacher, you may want to supplement his teachings with those of another.

If, however, you consult a second doctor who isn't as knowledgeable as the first, their diagnoses might conflict. The second doctor's medicine may counteract whatever healing has taken place, injuring your health. From one lama you may receive teachings on compassion and the four thoughts. You might then go to another who tells you that you don't need to do the preliminary practices. This will only undermine all the good advice given by the first lama. Even within the tradition of authentic lineage holders, there are teachers and there are teachers. A teacher–student relationship is like a mold: your realization will be only as great as your teacher's. Before you enter a relationship, make sure the teacher's qualities are ones you'd like to emulate.

Moving from teacher to teacher is like tearing seedling after seedling out of the ground and planting a new one each time. Your practice will never have a chance to mature; you'll keep disrupting the continuity necessary for the plant to grow. However, if throughout your practice, you maintain your commitment—in essence, to reduce the mind's poisons and increase love and compassion—then receiving additional teachings from other lamas will be like adding water and fertilizer to the seedling. Then it will grow and bear fruit.

If you're not benefiting from a particular teacher, there is no reason to continue studying with her. Nor should a teacher try to hold on to a student any more than a doctor should persist in treating a patient he can't help. It's better for the student to find a different teacher. There is no time in this brief human life to waste taking a direction that isn't productive.

QUESTION: Is it important to live near the lama?

RESPONSE: In the beginning stages of practice, proximity to the teacher is ideal. The lama functions as a mother, the student as an infant, the teachings as nourishment for the student. Just as a mother gives her child milk, the teacher gives the student teachings. Children receive continuous support, sustenance, correction, and guidance from their mother until they grow up and mature. Similarly, we are spiritual infants who need support and guidance, so the lama reminds us again and again of the methods and corrects us when we stray. Without a lama close by, it is hard to make progress, but whatever teachings and guidance we receive are better than none at all.

No one can always be with the lama. As our practice matures, it won't be as important to spend time with the outer, symbolic lama, because we can maintain our practice independently. Increasingly, we rely on the absolute lama within—our own true nature—as the teacher. But until we have gained some realization of the absolute lama, the symbolic lama remains essential.

QUESTION: Why is it important to pray to the lama when we practice?

RESPONSE: Blessings arise naturally and our qualities increase like the waxing moon through prayer to the lama and recognition that all aspects of practice—visualization, mantra recitation, and the dissolution of the visualization into emptiness—are the display of the lama's body, speech, and mind. With pure motivation and faith, we can swiftly accomplish the two stages of development and completion.

QUESTION: What does it mean to understand the deity as inseparable from the lama?

RESPONSE: In visualization practice, we understand that the essence of the deity and the essence of the lama are the same: all-pervasive wisdom. There are no boundaries between them. Similarly, even though we perceive a boundary enclosing our mind like a shell, our true nature is this same boundless wisdom.

The lama introduces us to the deity through empowerment and teachings. Due to the lama's blessings, our visualization practice enables us to reveal the qualities of the deity that exist naturally within us. So the lama is inseparable from all he gives us—inseparable from the deity and from the qualities that arise from practice. In that sense, the deity arises as the display of the lama's wisdom mind.

22

Introduction to Great Perfection

THE TEACHINGS OF the Great Perfection, or Dzogchen, the swiftest and most profound Buddhist path, are by tradition secret. They aren't freely revealed, because like snow lion's milk, they have to be held in a special container. In the past, the Great Perfection was presented only to people of the highest caliber, those almost awake. But such beings are very rare. Most of us need a developmental approach leading up to the teachings, for although we may be fortunate enough to have access to these teachings, we don't have the qualities or the aptitude to awaken effortlessly to mind's true nature.

For the fruition, the state of Great Perfection, to become evident through practice, one must follow a complete path unerringly in a step-by-step progression. If you were to build a car, you'd be careful to assemble all the parts correctly, to complete every electrical connection; otherwise it wouldn't run. Similarly, you must take great care in developing your spiritual vehicle, for mere exposure to these teachings doesn't guarantee enlightenment. If the mind isn't prepared, the transformation that comes through genuine transmission from Dzogchen master to student won't occur. Just as a seedling requires certain conditions to grow and bear fruit, we need to create conditions conducive to the full assimilation of the Great Perfection teachings. To do this, we use methods called the preliminary practices, or *ngondro*. Only then will the Great Perfection teachings have the fullest impact.

Receiving empowerment and completing the preliminaries are prerequisites for receiving Great Perfection teachings. The preliminary practices are like a bellows fanning a fire, causing it to blaze. These are not elementary practices that we only do when we start out on the spiritual path. They're like the ABCs we incorporate into every aspect of our education. The preliminaries connect us to dharma just as our obscurations connect us to samsara; they purify those obscurations and enhance our understanding all along the way. They incorporate every method we need to reveal mind's true nature.

We begin with the *ordinary preliminary practices:* contemplation of the four thoughts. People often think, "I've already heard the four thoughts." But in that case they've allowed them to become rote; they haven't penetrated to their meaning. These contemplations are essential to Great Perfection because they undercut samsaric attachment and engender enthusiasm for practice.

First, we contemplate the precious conditions we enjoy. These include the sacred spiritual methods available to us and the lama from whom we receive them, as well as our human body with its unparalleled capacity for spiritual accomplishment. We realize that this cherished opportunity won't last. Once impermanence intervenes and we lose this life, our karma won't disappear. Whether it will lead us toward liberation or further samsaric suffering depends on our practice.

We make a commitment, then, to take full advantage of this opportunity, and we pray that we will accomplish our purpose.

Then we drop all thoughts and allow the mind to rest, which leads our practice in the direction of Great Perfection meditation.

We might begin by devoting eighty percent of our practice to contemplation, twenty percent to resting the mind. When we start to experience less negativity and more enthusiasm for meditation, we know the contemplations are permeating our consciousness. Then we can let the mind rest for thirty percent, forty percent, fifty percent, or more of the time.

We prepare ourselves further through the *extraordinary preliminary practices*. We take refuge in the teacher, teachings, and lineage lamas of the rare and precious Great Perfection, reconfirming our bodhisattva commitment to follow in their footsteps along this extremely short path so that all beings might swiftly awaken to the glorious state of Great Perfection. In addition, we purify karma, gather merit, augment positive qualities, and rely with faith and devotion on the perfect teacher and teachings in order to deepen our awareness.

In my experience, there is a big difference in receptivity to Dzogchen teachings between one who has completed the preliminary practices and one who hasn't. There is also a difference between someone who has engaged in these practices diligently, with pure motivation and concentration, and someone who hasn't focused, who has simply repeated the mantra with a wandering mind.

In my area of Tibet, there lived a lama whose meditation seemed very good. He had done well in all the different categories of practice. But when it came to the Great Perfection, he simply couldn't understand the teachings—he hit a wall in meditation. So his teacher instructed him to recite the hundred-syllable mantra of Vajrasattva ten million times. He went into retreat and practiced day and night for nine years. When he came out, understanding arose effortlessly.

What is the significance of the term "Great Perfection" or "Great Completion," as Dzogchen is sometimes translated? What is it that we call perfect, complete? The true nature of mind is original purity, complete in and of itself—it needs no enhancing. When one tries to look at mind, there is nothing to find. Those without view will discover nothing, and neither will an enlightened being. Yet everything that arises is the display of mind, in no way separate from mind, just as waves are not separate from the ocean.

Within the nature of mind, samsara and nirvana are complete. Enlightenment itself is not beyond this nature. This completion —of all of samsara, of nirvana, of enlightenment itself—is the scope of Great Perfection. The *chen* in "Dzogchen" means "great," in that all beings throughout the three-thousand-fold universe have this complete, original purity.

If mind's true nature is complete or perfect, why do we suffer? Why do we need to meditate? We follow the path of Great Perfection because we don't see our perfection. Like heat melting ice, our practice dissolves the solid appearances of reality that obscure our essential nature, and the true qualities of mind become completely obvious.

So the foundation of Great Perfection is this great completion. The path is the process of removing that which obscures the foundational nature of mind. And the fruition is the complete realization of this nature, fully revealed.

In the Great Perfection approach, since the path is forged with awareness itself, we must differentiate between ordinary mind and awareness. Our intrinsic awareness in the present moment—

free of recollection, ordinary thought, artifice, or contrivance—is itself dharmakaya, the enlightened intent of original purity. This is directly introduced in the immediacy of our own true nature as self-occurring pristine awareness, or wisdom. Beyond the three times of past, present, and future, we come to a decision in the immediacy of this experience. Self-arising and self-freeing, like waves resolving back into the ocean, recollections and thoughts resolve into the ground of being, leaving no trace. We gain an inner confidence in the immediacy of this freedom.

When we are immersed in that unwavering state, our appreciation for and enjoyment of phenomenal reality enhance our realization, a process termed *conduct*. These and other aspects of this approach must be heard in more detail directly from a qualified lama.

The highest view must be combined with impeccable action. Then our practice becomes infallible. We can talk about buddha nature and emptiness, but without realization our words alone won't create transformation. We need to be very honest about our capability. A fox mustn't think it can leap as far as a lion, even if it can see the goal. If we don't have profound realization of the true nature of reality, we must be extremely careful in our actions. We can't discount our relative experience, thinking it doesn't matter because everything is empty. We must remain attentive to it until we attain enlightenment.

As practitioners we're very young, like kindergartners. We mustn't drink poison, whether the nature of that poison is empty or not. We may be students of Great Perfection, but if our understanding is incomplete, our thoughts, speech, and actions negative, we'll still make negative karma. The Great Perfection won't liberate us. We'll just get more deeply entrenched in samsara. Until we have attained stable realization, everything we do, think, or say counts. The great master Padmasambhava said, "In my tradition, one's view is as high as the sky and one's actions as fine as barley flour."

Acting with great care, meditating, and maintaining view bring maturity to practice and accelerate progress on the path. Shantideva said that if we know mind's true nature directly and maintain that knowing, all dualistic experience will be conquered and all poisons of the mind purified. If you are doing great practice, you'll notice changes day by day. If your practice isn't that effective, change will occur week by week, month by month, or year by year. If there is no change at all, even after years of meditation, the fault lies with the quality of your practice. You can't blame the dharma.

These days, though many people talk about Great Perfection, few achieve the level of realization of past practitioners. Not as many attain rainbow body, the dissolution of the body's elements into light upon the attainment of enlightenment. People say they are practicing Great Perfection, yet haven't even accomplished the basics of reducing anger, attachment, and ignorance.

The problem doesn't lie in the teachings themselves, nor has the mind-to-mind lineage been broken. It's that practitioners aren't diligent. One can't simply choose a teaching, practice as much of it as one likes, and ignore the rest. It doesn't work that way. It is essential to persist in one's efforts from the very foundation to completion.

We may receive great teachings and methods, but if we don't make use of them, we're like someone amassing money that won't cross the threshold of death—we're just wasting time. If we practice Great Perfection diligently, we can attain enlightenment within seven years, or with more diligence, purity, and receptivity, within three years, or even one. Without such qualities, we can sit in retreat for sixteen or thirty-two years, our minds racing, and achieve nothing at all. Our retreat hut will just feel like a jail. Or we can practice each moment of the day in the midst of worldly activities, directing the mind to dharma, resting in awareness, and attain enlightenment in this very lifetime.

Though fully aware that they are illusory, a bodhisattva undertakes effortful meditation and performs beneficial activities for the sake of those trapped by their belief in a seemingly solid reality. This leads to the fruition of the path: the complete realization of one's foundational nature, the all-completing Great Perfection. Through the full accomplishment of view, meditation, and action, beneficial activity arises spontaneously.

QUESTION: I've had some experiences in meditation that make me wonder if I've already seen the nature of mind. If so, is it still necessary to do the preliminary practices in order to receive the Great Perfection teachings?

RESPONSE: Getting a glimpse of your true nature is just a first step; that experience has to be stabilized. We may have an idea that there is something wonderful at the top of a staircase, and may even have caught sight of it, but if we have never actually walked up the stairs, we won't know how to make it to the top or how to remain there. If we think we already know what's there, we might never bother to climb the steps at all. It is important that we practice the methods that can give rise to realization of the resplendent qualities of our true nature. There are a few fortunate beings with extraordinary karma who can jump directly to the top floor, but most of us need to climb the stairs, step by step.

It's easy to talk about mind's nature, but not to experience it directly. Intellectual understanding does not bring realization. At first it's difficult to even recognize awareness. Once we have removed some layers of obscuration, we may taste it, but we still aren't able to stabilize our recognition. We may believe that body, speech, and mind are empty, but when someone says something nasty, anger—not wisdom—arises.

The preliminary practices provide a sure method of purifying the habitual patterns that delude us and prevent us from recognizing our true nature. Without having done the preliminaries, a student can listen to the Great Perfection teachings, but they won't take hold, just as a seed cannot take root in dry ground. There will be no profound transformation, so the student might lose faith in the dharma and enthusiasm for practice, thinking that what she has received is no big deal.

Once a student told me that he had completed the preliminary practices, so I gave him permission to attend a Great Perfection retreat. Most of the students at the retreat experienced a genuine taste of the Great Perfection. Although this student claimed that he knew all kinds of things, it was apparent to me that he had received nothing from the teachings. I told him that I doubted he had done the preliminaries. He insisted he had, but two years later he confessed to me that he had lied, and made a commitment to complete the practices before attending another Great Perfection retreat.

A genuine experience of mind's nature is subtle and delicate; ordinary effort won't lead to it, nor will ideas capture it. It is often said that it's too easy to believe. We tend to think it's something more dramatic than it is. With proper preparation through the preliminary practices, a student who has been introduced to the highest teachings and has had that experience will definitely progress on the path. How quickly depends on the student's diligence and skill.

QUESTION: How can effortful practice prepare us for the effortless practice of Great Perfection?

RESPONSE: We need to begin where we are. We have concepts, so we use concepts to cut concepts. We have hope and fear, so we use them to take us beyond hope and fear. Fear of sickness and hope for a cure inspire us to take medicine. Similarly, fear of suffering and hope for happiness inspire us to undertake the effortful practice that will purify our ordinary habits. This will bring us to the effortless practice of the Great Perfection, resting in mind's true nature, free of hope and fear. Just as we bend a warped piece of wood in the opposite direction in order to straighten it, we bend the mind away from its habitual delusion so that we can realize the natural state.

We use effortful practice to refine away the dualistic habits of ordinary mind. At first the mind remains steeped in that duality, so only an effortful approach will work. Yet we also need to relax effortlessly into a state in which delusion, habit, and obscuration are swiftly freed in their own ground. In the beginning, such moments of resting genuinely in awareness are few and far between. So we alternate skillfully between effortful contemplation and effortless resting—development and completion stage practice—to cut our attachment to either one and achieve an equilibrium in which we can realize mind's true nature.

23

Mind of Activity, Nature of Mind

IN THE BUDDHIST TRADITION, we distinguish between intellectual understanding, unstable experience, and stable realization. Intellectual understanding, like a poorly stitched patch that eventually falls off, is temporary. If we go further in our practice, we may have a glimpse of the true nature of mind, but like mist, it will dissipate. What we are working toward is an unalterable realization, like space itself, which by its very nature never changes.

When our understanding of impermanence and the illusory quality of existence increases, we begin to observe phenomena without projecting our false assumptions. With time, we come to recognize open, naked awareness as our true nature and the true nature of reality.

To get to this experience of what is natural, start by acknowledging impermanence in every action of your body, every word of your speech, every movement of your mind. As you move your hand, recognize its changing position as a demonstration of impermanence: first it was on the left, then on the right. Recognize impermanence in your breath as it comes in and goes out. With practice, the deliberate intellectual process of looking at each thing and thinking, "This is impermanent," evolves into a natural, uncontrived knowing of the ongoing display of change.

This softens our stance toward reality; we begin to appreciate the truth of the Buddha's metaphors comparing phenomena to illusions or dream images, hallucinations, echoes, or rainbows— apparent but not tangible or corporeal—like reflections of the moon in water, brilliant yet insubstantial.

Our current understanding is based on inherited assumptions, dependent on ordinary ways of perceiving. We have been taught to name things, investing them with a reality they don't have. Ordinary mind is very discursive, clicking through one thought after another. We may believe we're multifaceted, mosaic-like thinkers, but we're just very quick changers. All the concepts and thoughts that arise in the mind—in fact, our whole experience of reality—aren't much different than a drawing traced on the surface of water. Even as the image is created, it is no longer there.

Belief in the solidity of experience produces attachment and aversion, which in turn perpetually fuel the fire of samsara, until our reality resembles a raging inferno. When we understand the truth of our experience, we stop feeding the fire. While the flames don't immediately disappear, the fire slowly dies out. Without attachment and aversion, we aren't confused by the push and pull of phenomena. In the clear space of the mind between thoughts—in that natural openness—is awareness.

Great practitioners have attained enlightenment by continually bringing awareness to their work. All day long for twelve years, the Indian master Tilopa pounded sesame seeds to make oil. With each movement, his awareness remained fully present; it didn't slip off into past or future, into flights of fancy. The same was true of Togtzepa, a practitioner who dug ditches; with each movement, he maintained awareness.

Similarly, many of India's eighty-four mahasiddhas, highly

realized practitioners, worked at ordinary jobs. As they labored, they meditated. By resting in awareness in the midst of their activities—no matter what they did—they developed the ability to transform fire into water, water into fire, to walk through walls and fly through the air. Rather than remaining subject to ordinary reality, they became its master. Of course, it's not the purpose of meditation to change water into fire, but such extraordinary abilities are a natural by-product of cutting our clinging to ordinary perceptions of reality.

Once a king's son went to a yogi for meditation instructions. After the yogi had shown him a method, the boy said, "This won't work for me. But I do know music. Is there a meditation I can do while playing my instrument?"

"Remember as you play," the yogi replied, "that sound is emptiness and emptiness is sound. Sound is not beyond emptiness; emptiness is not beyond sound."

We, too, can change the mind swiftly if we bring awareness to all of our activities. When you build, keep your mind present with each strike of the hammer. Don't let thoughts intervene. As you write, keep your mind present with each stroke of the pen. Don't let it jump around. When you chop wood, maintain awareness with each swing of the ax. Whatever you do, relax your mind—gently rest in openness, immersed in what is going on, fully present, but at the same time conscious of the play of phenomena. An adult watching children in the park never loses awareness of the fact that they're playing, yet she doesn't deliberately focus on their activities, thinking, "They're playing, they're playing, they're playing."

We often lose this relaxation of the mind when we're completely consumed by our work—for example, when we're so involved in writing that we're almost inside the words. In allowing the mind to rest, there is more space. It's like being a little outside of what is happening, aware that it's a display, but without distancing ourselves and establishing duality.

The lives of great practitioners consistently show that to maintain one's practice of the dharma, it is not necessary to renounce the world. Nor does one have to renounce the dharma in order to maintain worldly involvement. It's possible to integrate both into one's life. Gradually, new priorities and a necessary balance will emerge.

In my time, I've witnessed four people attain rainbow body upon their death, and they didn't live in monasteries—they were householders. When I was twenty-two, I saw a person attain rainbow body; most people didn't even know he'd been doing spiritual practice. There is no need to make an outer display to succeed on the spiritual path. It's not our body we change to become enlightened—it's the mind.

You can adopt a hermit's lifestyle, give up your concern for food, clothing, wealth, friends, family, and home, go off into the hills, and devote yourself entirely to formal meditation. That is one perfectly valid way to practice, but in the Vajrayana there is another. You don't leave home, renounce anything, or change your outer life. However, you are never separate from virtue, from dharma, from the intention to benefit, or from awareness.

Tilopa said to his student Naropa, "You are bound not by appearances, but by your clinging to them, so cut through that clinging, Naropa." We are bound to samsara not because we have possessions, high status, or friends, but because we cling to them.

You have to practice consistently, right where the mind is active, right there with the experience of desire, anger, or happiness, at each moment. Then your meditation and your work join in a kind of marriage. If you want swift results, it's not enough to meditate only an hour or two a day. Never think, "I'll work now and meditate later." Who knows if you'll live that long? The lord of death is hard to put off. When he comes to visit, he won't listen if you say, "I'm sorry, but I've been so busy, and now I need to meditate. Just give me a week, a month, or three years."

Through devoted practice, we develop the ability to transform negative conditions into supportive ones. We call this "carrying adversity onto the path"—not allowing obstacles to block, sway, or overwhelm us, but rather seeing them as opportunities for practice. The entire phenomenal world then acts as a teacher, helping us to develop skill in dealing with life. Everything that happens to us becomes a part of the path. Trials turn into opportunities for practice because they force us to develop patience. We learn to accept adversity joyously because we understand that our suffering purifies karma. A single headache can purify what would be hundreds of years of suffering in a hell realm. This doesn't mean we reject happiness; rather, we rejoice in it, dedicate our merit to others, and pray that their happiness will last.

Sometimes people learning to meditate tell me that it's hopeless, that their thoughts are impossible to control. I assure them that this is a sign of improvement. Their mind has always been unruly; it's just that they're finally noticing it. In the past, they've let it wander freely, following whatever stream of thought occurred. But now that they're more aware of what goes on in the mind, they can begin to change.

You may complain that meditation isn't easy. But remember that you're leading your mind, like a wild horse, into the corral of awareness. You'll know that your practice is working if you're not so dominated by your emotions and confusion, if you bring to whatever you are doing—wherever you are—openness, relaxation, and compassionate intention, remaining aware of the play of the mind and of the nature of everything taking place around you.

Once a student who was having problems meditating came to the Buddha. When the Buddha asked how he made a living, the man replied that he was a lute player. The Buddha asked, "When you tune your lute, do you set the strings tightly or leave them loose?" The man answered, "Neither. If I leave them too tight or too loose, I get the wrong tones." He'd answered his own question about meditation. Whether in our practice or in our work, we need to maintain a balance, being neither too tense and attached, nor too loose and sloppy.

Once a fine lama had a rather dense student who asked obvious questions but never quite understood the answers. One day the teacher, in great frustration, looked at him and said, "But you don't have horns"—meaning "You're not a cow; you should be able to understand what I say."

The student, still not comprehending, thought the teacher meant that he *should* have horns. Taking this to heart, he went into retreat, and every day he visualized himself with horns. Three years later the teacher asked his attendant, "Whatever happened to that student of mine who wasn't very bright?" When told the student was in retreat meditating, the lama exclaimed, "How can he be meditating? He doesn't know anything. Bring him to me."

So a messenger was sent to fetch the student. Arriving at the retreat cave, he peeked through the small door and saw the student sitting there with a lovely set of horns. The messenger called, "Your teacher wants to see you; please come."

The student stood up to leave, but couldn't get those huge horns through the door. He told the messenger, "Please extend my great apologies to my teacher. I would come, but I can't get out of the cave because of my horns."

On hearing this, the teacher said, "That is wonderful! Now tell him to meditate on not having horns."

Through the power of his concentration, the student removed the horns in seven days and returned to the lama. The lama then gave him proper meditation instructions, and he very quickly attained realization.

People give many reasons for not doing spiritual practice. Some say they don't believe the teachings; others feel they're not ready or don't have the capability. But they are mistaken. Whether or not we believe in samsara, this is where we are. Whether or not we believe in karma, we are creating it. Whether or not we believe in the poisons of the mind, they exist. What is the benefit of not believing in medicine? Whether we are ready to do practice or not, death and sickness won't wait. Why not prepare? Why not develop the capability to help ourselves and others? We're ready to drink poison but not to take medicine.

Not meditating once we've received teachings is like shopping for all our favorite foods, arranging them beautifully in the kitchen, and then not eating. We'll starve to death. Meditating is like eating: our pantry is full and we partake of what we've gathered. Instead of telling ourselves, "I don't have time today, I'll meditate tomorrow. I don't have time this week, I'll do it next week. This is a busy year, I'll get around to it next year," we need to feel an urgency about doing practice—not just today, not just this hour, but this very moment.

Now let us dedicate all the virtue of these teachings, of the changes we will make from having been exposed to these truths, and of the changes others will undergo by having seen us enact what we have learned. I pray that each and every being's true nature be revealed, that we each see clearly our inherent truth and find liberation from the shackles of suffering and sorrow imposed by the limitations of ordinary mind.

So it flows out, in rings of benefit.

Glossary

Non-English entries are Sanskrit terms, unless otherwise indicated.

Abhidharma one of the collections of the Buddha's teachings; serving as antidotes to ignorance, these teachings discuss logic, psychology, and cosmology

absolute truth the pure, immutable essence of phenomena; also refers to the true nature of mind

Amitabha the buddha of limitless light, whose aspirations and dedication of merit facilitate rebirth in his pureland, Dewachen

anu yoga the category of practice in the Nyingma school of Vajrayana in which one works with the channels, energies, and bindu of the subtle body to realize the true nature of desire and the inseparability of bliss and emptiness

ati yoga *See* Great Perfection

bardo(s) (Tib.; lit. "interval between two points") the six intermediate states of cyclic existence; often refers exclusively to the intermediate state between death and rebirth

bindu (Tib. *tiglé*) concentration of energies in the subtle body, which one works with in the training of anu yoga

bodhicitta (Tib. *jang chub sem;* lit. "mind of enlightenment") on the relative level, it involves arousing compassion equally for all beings and the wish to attain buddhahood for their sake, as well as engaging in practice and activity in order to achieve this; on the absolute level, it is awareness of the true nature of reality

bodhisattva a practitioner on the Mahayana path whose goal is enlightenment and whose sole motivation is the immediate and ultimate benefit of all beings

buddha (Tib. *sang gyay*) one who has removed all obscurations and given rise to all positive qualities, including the two forms of omniscience: complete knowledge of past, present, and future causes and conditions as well as the true nature of reality; the first of the Three Jewels of refuge

buddha nature the fundamentally pure nature of mind, which in all beings constitutes the basis for attaining enlightenment

Buddha Shakyamuni (fifth century B.C.E.) the fourth of the thousand buddhas to appear in this eon; he attained enlightenment at Bodh Gaya, India, and taught the 84,000 methods of the Buddhadharma

channels pathways by which energy circulates in the subtle body, which one works with in the training of anu yoga

clear light lucid aspect of mind's true nature, free of any obscuring overlay; sometimes refers to the experience of pristine awareness that occurs momentarily in the initial stage of the intermediate state between death and rebirth

completion stage in maha yoga visualization, the stage of dissolving the visualization generated in the development stage and resting effortlessly in mind's true nature; the anu yoga practices of working with the channels, energies, and bindu of the subtle body; the ati yoga practice of resting in awareness

dakini the feminine aspect of mind's true nature; also, a great female practitioner; the third of the Three Roots of refuge, the source of enlightened activity and auspicious circumstances

development stage in maha yoga visualization, the stage involving effort in which one generates the clear visualization of a deity, recites mantra, and rests in nondual awareness

Dewachen (Tib.; lit. "great bliss") Buddha Amitabha's pureland

dharma the body of teachings of the Buddha Shakyamuni, which includes the 84,000 methods for revealing mind's true nature and attaining enlightenment; the second of the Three Jewels of refuge

dharma protector (*dharmapala;* Tib. *gonpo*) a worldly or enlightened being pledged to guard Vajrayana practitioners against obstacles and protect the Buddhist teachings from dilution or distortion

dharmakaya the sphere of absolute truth; the essence of mind as emptiness

dharmata the true nature of reality

dream yoga a meditation method in which one trains in recognition of the dream state and then uses that state to further one's spiritual development

dualistic perception the perception that reality is divided into subject (self) and object (other), each with an independent identity

empowerment a ceremony during which a qualified lama introduces a student to his or her true nature as the body, speech, and mind of the deity, authorizes the student to meditate on the mandala of the deity, and transmits the blessings of the practice lineage

emptiness the essence of mind; also, the lack of inherent existence of self and phenomena

enlightenment buddhahood; the awakened state of mind in which all obscurations have been purified and all enlightened qualities revealed

five poisons negative emotions that lead to rebirth in the realms of samsara: anger or aversion, pride, desire, jealousy, and ignorance

five wisdoms (five aspects of pristine awareness) mirror-like wisdom, wisdom of equanimity, discriminating wisdom, all-accomplishing wisdom, and wisdom of the basic space of phenomena

four immeasurable qualities limitless equanimity, love, compassion, and joy

four kinds of activity four kinds of enlightened activity that arise spontaneously from realization of mind's true nature: pacifying, increasing, magnetizing, and wrathful

four obscurations factors that prevent one from recognizing mind's true nature: intellectual obscuration; the poisons of the mind, or emotional obscurations; karma; and habit

four powers of confession essential supports for the purification of a negative action: an enlightened being as one's witness; sincere regret; a firm commitment never to repeat the action; and the blessing of purification from the enlightened being

four thoughts precious human birth, impermanence, karma, and suffering; contemplation of these thoughts turns the mind toward spiritual teachings and practice

Great Perfection (Tib. Dzogchen) ati yoga; the most profound category of Vajrayana practice according to the Nyingma school, in which awareness of mind's true nature constitutes the path, leading to realization of the inseparability of awareness and emptiness

guru yoga the method of Vajrayana in which one relies on one's relationship with a lama to achieve liberation, blending one's mind with the enlightened mind of the lama, which is inseparable from one's own true nature

Hinayana the Buddhist approach of personal liberation in which one seeks freedom from samsara through renunciation and cutting worldly attachments

karma principle of infallible cause and effect whereby virtue creates happiness and nonvirtue creates suffering

lama (Tib.; Skt. *guru*) in Vajrayana, the spiritual teacher, who demonstrates the path to enlightenment and provides instruction and guidance; the first of the Three Roots of refuge, the root of blessings

lineage the unbroken line of spiritual transmission, generation to generation, from a fully awakened buddha

maha yoga the category in the Nyingma school of Vajrayana that emphasizes the visualization of deities and mandalas, mantra repetition, and other methods to purify one's ordinary perception and bring about realization of the inseparability of form and emptiness

mahasiddha (lit. "greatly accomplished master") often refers to eighty-four masters who lived in ancient India and gained spiritual realization in the course of ordinary worldly activities

Mahayana the spiritual path of one whose motivation for attaining enlightenment is to free all beings from samsara and establish them in the state of buddhahood

mandala any configuration of enlightened mind—for example, the outer mandala of the three-thousand-fold universe, the inner mandala of the subtle channels, energies, and bindu, or the secret mandala of the three kayas; also, a sacred art form depicting the display and qualities of enlightened mind

mantra a reference to the "secret mantra approach" (the Vajrayana); syllables, usually in Sanskrit, that embody the deity's enlightened speech; signifies "that which protects the practitioner's mind," i.e., from negativity and confused thinking

mara (lit. "deadening influence") anything that obstructs one's attainment of enlightenment

nirmanakaya an embodiment of enlightened mind manifesting in a physical form to benefit beings who are unable to perceive the pure expression of the sambhogakaya

nirvana state beyond the suffering of samsara; on the most exalted level, complete enlightenment beyond both samsara and nirvana

Padmasambhava also known as Guru Rinpoche, the Indian master who established the Vajrayana teachings in Tibet in the ninth century; revered by many as the "second Buddha"

p'howa (Tib.) transference of consciousness to a pure realm of experience at the time of death

preliminaries (Tib. *ngondro*) foundational practices of the Vajrayana undertaken to purify obscurations, accumulate merit, and awaken realization of mind's true nature

pureland, pure realm realm of purity manifested by a buddha in which there is no suffering and enlightenment is ensured

rainbow body dissolution of the body's elements into light upon enlightenment

refuge the first formal step in entering the Buddhist path; the commitment to turn away from the causes of suffering and turn toward the infallible sources of immediate and ultimate benefit for all beings

relative truth the appearance of phenomena on a conventional level, which the ordinary mind believes to have inherent existence

rupakaya (lit. "form kaya") the manifest aspects of enlightened mind, including the sambhogakaya and nirmanakaya

samaya in the Vajrayana, the indispensable bond of commitment forged between the lama and student; also, the student's commitment to uphold vows of practice taken at the time of empowerment

sambhogakaya the pure expression of enlightened mind perceptible only to highly realized practitioners

samsara the endless cycles of birth and death within the six realms, which are pervaded by suffering

sangha (Tib. *gendun;* lit. "those who love virtue") those who practice, realize, and uphold the teachings of the Buddha and function as companions and guides on the Buddhist path; the third of the Three Jewels of refuge

shamata (Tib. *zhinay*) calm abiding; one of two major methods of Buddhist meditation, in which the mind rests one-pointedly, without distraction

six perfections (*paramitas*) qualities perfected by a bodhisattva that support the practice of the Mahayana path: generosity, moral discipline, patience, diligence, concentration, and wisdom

six realms the realities experienced by beings caught in samsara due to fundamental confusion concerning the true nature of mind as well as a predominant mental poison: the realms of hell beings (anger or hatred), hungry ghosts (miserliness or greed), animals (ignorance), humans (a mixture of poisons), demigods (jealousy), and gods (pride)

spiritual accomplishment (*siddhi;* Tib. *ngödrup*) on the most sublime level, the attainment of enlightenment; also, supernormal powers that are by-products of spiritual practice

subtle energies energies of the subtle body, which one works with in the training of anu yoga

Sutra one of the collections of the Buddha's teachings; serving as antidotes to anger, these teachings constitute the Buddha's discourses on a variety of subjects

Three Collections of Dharma (Tripitaka) the Buddha's teachings categorized as Vinaya, Sutra, and Abhidharma

three elements (or stages) of faith a feeling of awe toward the spiritual teacher and teachings; a desire to emulate the teacher and to study and practice the teachings; and an unwavering conviction, based on practice, in the teacher and teachings

Three Jewels the Buddha as the teacher, the dharma as the teachings, and the sangha as the community of practitioners; the outer sources of refuge

three kayas three aspects of the totality of enlightened mind; the secret sources of refuge (*see* dharmakaya, sambhogakaya, and nirmanakaya)

three kinds of suffering as taught by the Buddha Shakyamuni, the suffering of change, suffering atop suffering, and the pervasive suffering inherent in samsara

three realms a categorization of samsara, in which beings are trapped due to fundamental confusion concerning the true nature of mind: the desire realm, the form realm, and the formless realm

Three Roots the lama, the root of blessings; the yidam, or chosen deity, the root of spiritual accomplishment; and the dakini, the root of enlightened activity and auspicious circumstances; the inner sources of refuge

three spheres subject, object, and the action between them; belief in their inherent existence constitutes the domain of relative truth

tonglen (Tib. lit. "sending and receiving") meditation used in the development of bodhicitta

tulku (Tib.; Skt. nirmanakaya) the incarnation of a former spiritual master who has taken rebirth intentionally to benefit others

two accumulations on the relative level, the accumulation of merit through the development of compassion and skillful means; on the absolute level, the accumulation of wisdom through direct perception of the true nature of reality

two kinds of benefit that which benefits oneself, the realization of dharmakaya; and that which benefits others, the manifestation of the form kaya; also, immediate and ultimate benefit

vajra refers to the immutable nature of body, speech, and mind

Vajrayana the spiritual path of those who follow the Mahayana approach and who also employ a wide variety of skillful methods; involves developing and maintaining a pure view of reality

view knowledge of the true nature of reality which leads to complete realization of that nature beyond concepts

Vinaya one of the collections of the Buddha's teachings; serving as antidotes to desire, these teachings discuss discipline and ethical conduct, particularly in the monastic context

vipashyana (Tib. *lhagtong;* lit. "deeper insight") one of two major methods of Buddhist meditation, in which one develops insight into the true nature of mind and phenomena

visualization in Vajrayana, the practice of visualizing oneself as a deity and one's environment as a pureland in order to purify ordinary dualistic perception; one ultimately realizes one's true nature as that of the deity

wisdom understanding of the true nature of mind; awareness as the direct realization of that nature

yana spiritual approach or vehicle; the three categories of Hinayana, Mahayana, and Vajrayana are further divided into nine yanas

yidam (Tib.) a meditation deity (or "chosen deity") that a practitioner relies on for spiritual accomplishment; the second of the Three Roots of refuge

Index